Truth Warriors

Franklin Ysaac

October 2022

Published in USA by

TATAY JOBO ELIZES,
*Self-Publisher, under the
permission and authorization of*

Franklin Ysaac
author and copyright owner

The copyright owner can withdraw this permission at his discretion without any objection from Talay Jobo Elizes at any time. Printing of this book is using the present day method of Print-On-Demand (POD) system, where prints will never run out of copies to be available for posterity. The copyright owner is free to republish with other publishers anytime.

**KDP ISBN: 9798358187788
Independently Published**

Contact: job_elizes@yahoo.com +
https://www.facebook.com/franklin.ysaac +
http://tinyurl.com/mj76ccq (amazon site) +
www.tatayjoboelizes.webs.com +
https://www.facebook.com/groups/399368500835109

Contents

1—Update – Aug. 18, 2022 - Know about Franklin Ysaac - *p6*

2— Update - Aug. 17, 2022 - Comelec unresponsive - *p11*

3— Update -Aug. 18, 2022 – Leo Paras Lettter – *p13*

4-- Update – Aug. 19, 2022 – 2 Months Already – *p15*

5-- Update – Aug. 19, 2022, 9M – Comelec Letter – - *p17*

6—Update - Aug. 23, 2022 – Cabinet Members – *p20*

7—Update - August 25, 2022 – Support Petition – *p27*

8—Update - Aug. 28, 2022 – Need for Prayer – *p28*

9—Update - Aug. 28, 2022 – TruthWarriorPrayer = - - *p30*

10-- Update – Aug. 29, 2022 - Forensic Science – *p31*

11—Update - Aug. 31, 2022 – Student Election System – *p37*

12—Update - Sep. 1, 2022 – Economic Outlook – *p40*

13-- Update - Sep. 1, 2022, 2PM – Slow Progress – - *p42*

14—Update - Sep 1, 2022 6PM – Art of War by Sun Tzu – *p44*

15—Update - Sep. 2, 2022, 7AM – Forex Rate – *p45*

16—Update - Sept. 3, 2022 – Directory – *p48*

17—Update – Sept. 4, 2022 - Sunday -
   Homily – Clairevouyers – *p60*

18—Update - Sept. 9, 2022 – Mystery Novels – *p63*

19—Update - Sept. 18, 2022 – Hiding the Truth – *p65*

20—Update - Sept. 19, 2022 – On One's Faith – *p67*

21—Update - Sept. 19, 2022 – Trips abroad – *p69*

22—Update - Sept. 20, 2022 - 10AM NYC –
   Mandamus Petition to SC – *p71*

23—Update - Sept. 20, 2022, 10PM NYC –
   Transparency Lack – *p73*

24—Update - Sept. 21, 2022, 11AM, NYC time –
   PPCRV – (Parish Pastoral Council for
   Responsible Voting) – *p75*

25—Update - Sept. 24, 2022 – cavaliers' Letters
   (Military) – *p79*

26—Update – Sept. 27, 2022 - 10PM NY Time -
   Meaning of Mandamus Petition – *p84*

27—Update - Sep. 29, 8PM, NYC – No Politics – *p89*

28—Update – Update - Oct. 1, 2022, 9AM, NYC time
   Strong Dollars – *p90*

29—Update - Oct. 7, 2022, 9AM – About CBCP and
   PPCRV – *p93*

30—Update - Oct. 7, 2022 – 7PM NYC -
      Something fishy about the CBCP and PPCRV
      And the Runaround tactics – *p95*

31—Update - Oct. 8, 2022, NYC 11AM –
      Letter to Truth Warriors – *p98*

32—Update - Oct. 9, 2022, NYC time, 9PM –
      Faith in our Cause – *p100*

33—Update - Oct. 11, 2022, NYC time, 130PM –
      Personal Experience in Banking - *p104*

34—Update - Oct. 11, 2022, NYC time, 6PM –
      What about whistleblowers – *p108*

35—Update - Oct. 12, 2022 NYC time 6PM –
      Our Case for Truth Imnproving – *p109*

36—Update - Oct. 13, 2022, NYC time 700PM –
      Brave Lawyers - *p111*

oooooo

1
Update - Aug. 18, 2022
Know a Little about the Author, Franklin Ysaac

May I digress for a few minutes from my usual post about the election, as my sister, Sor Norma Ysaac of the Daughters of Charity just called me to remind me about the death anniversary of our father, retired M/Sgt Luis Ysaac, PS of the US Army.

He passed away 56 years ago when I was just 16 and I was graduating from HS at Ateneo de Naga.

My father, like many of us when we were young, inspired us to become leaders on our own, to succeed on our own, and not to be dependent on others. But like many parents, my father who served the US Army for more than 30 years wanted me to join the US Armed Forces. Drawing inspiration from him, I was chosen to become the PMT corps cmdr and led the Ateneo batallion in competitions amongst PMT corps from different schools.

But before the final competition which was going to be held during the Penafrancia fiesta celebration in September, my father got sick and after one month in the hospital in Manila, he succumbed to kidney failure.

At 16 years and graduating, I suddenly felt lost as my military option didn't push through.

After soul searching, I decided to take the entrance exam at UP and took the foreign service career as my dream shifted from military career to a lawyer diplomat career.

But the four years I spent in UP were full of political changes and demonstrations from students against the president who had already become a strongman. His first four years (1965-69) became hotbed of opposition from congress and the students became politicized. After his re-election in 1969, the president became even ruthless as demonstrations against his term became stronger. The left was already getting into the streets almost daily and the quarter storm was one of the days when he was already contemplating imposing martial law and suspension of habeas corpus. Many of the student leaders were then targeted by the military and were arrested, incarcerated and tortured by the dreaded Metrocom.

During the Diliman commune where I was active as member of the Arts and Sciences student council, we held ourselves up in the AS bldg and the Metrocom units were preparing to attack us from the Engineering bldg. As night fell, we heard sounds of gunfire and we saw tracer bullets whizzing through our bldg. We managed to escape from the back and ran towards Katipunan. After that fateful day, we heard about some of the barrikada students were wounded from gunshots.

It was a tumultuous day and when my mother learned about that incident, she refused to send me back to UP.

The UP campus became a garrison as student leaders began to flee from the campus and many went underground.

I managed to finish my studies when things calmed down but since the military was still present in the campus, the UP President called off our graduation exercises as protests were still brewing again.

Those were the dark days before martial law was declared the following year.

Perhaps, my father's choice of me joining the US Armed forces was not meant for me. My other career to become a lawyer diplomat was also frozen because my mother refused to send me back to UP.

Not knowing where I was going, I applied for a masters program in business at Ateneo Padre Faura. The placement bureau director helped me with an endorsement to apply either at Bank of America or FNCB. After passing the exams from both banks, I chose FNCB and I never looked back.

I was just in my first year there when martial law was declared the following year. Because of the presence of many soldiers and with the free press muzzled, there was no way you can get information. Curfew was imposed and all civil liberties were banned.

The movie, Katips, showed every aspect of the life then and it's unfortunate that the young generation couldn't believe what happened then. In fact, because of disinformation, the successor son called those years the golden age . Yes, I agree. Those were years where the Golden Buddha was supposed to have been discovered from the treasure kept by the Japanese invaders.

Tomorrow, August 19, and a Friday, at early morning hours, my father was called to heaven.

With my father gone, I was left alone to carve my destiny. From a law diplomat career to a banker to an IT, that was the long road I took.

Is it destiny that I became an IT activist when I started posting in my Fb account my questions about the election result?

Is it my destiny to be followed by frustrated followers of the running candidate who was the chosen one?

Is it my destiny to be joined by a former Comelec commissioner and former Namfrel chairman and former DICT Usec to become #TNTrio.

Is it our destiny that because of our relentless campaign for truth and transparency, we are now getting closer to the truth?

But destiny is not in our hands.

Just like during the snap and Edsa revolution, our prayers were answered.

Let's continue with our prayers storming the heavens and the good Lord to protect and guide us again to achieve our goal - to know the whole truth so we can be free again, free from corruption, and from free from want.

To my father, thank you for nurturing me to become an honest citizen and that's your legacy to me and that's my legacy to my children.

In my clip here which I lifted from my album, I am proud to show a picture of my father together with my mother during their wedding and my picture as PMT corps cmdr.

The four highest officers in Tikas Pahinga
Cdt. Maj. Franklin Ysaac, S-1 Cdt. Capt. Efren Badong, S-2 Cdt. Capt. Danilo Borjal,
Cdt. Capt. Roberto Totanes

oooooo

2
Update, Aug. 17, 2022
Comelec unresponsive

In the interest of our drive to ferret out the truth from the probable irregularities in the May election, we the #TNTrio has always kept the door open so you will all know our movements when we raise questions about these irregularities.

We never kept you in the dark and we will uphold our sovereign right to know the truth.

We don't have the power of the governing body but we cannot allow nor accept the untruths.

Our July 15 letter was an eye opener as we asked for the release of the transmission data from vcm to transparency server. We conducted thoroughly simulated transactions from casting of ballots to production of ERs and several copies to the actual transmission of ERs via telcos to the transparency server and we couldn't accept their explanation that the election was the fastest in the history of our election.

Comelec's response dated August 15 to our letter did not answer our request. Their answer was unacceptable to us as they referred us to the two bodies, Comelec Advisory Council and the Joint Cingressional Oversight Committee on Automated Election System.

In our prepared response to their August 15 letter, we are expressing our displeasure on their referral of their answer to the two bodies. To us, such referral was administrative but the real transmission data including the CDRs or call detail reports from telcos are still in their hands. What they submitted to the two bodies are just copies of the original documents which are supposed to be kept in a safe place.

Hence, in our response letter, we will still insist that they deliver to us records of these data. Otherwise, we will be constrained to raise this matter to the higher body which is the Supreme Court.

Even if this ping pong battle or back and forth fight for the truth takes us longer than we expected, we will hold our ground.

In this effort to secure the data, we enjoin the #truthwarriors yesterday to do their share of individually writing the same request to the Comelec. This won't take much of your time as you can write your own letter with the guidance or format we published here and it's going to cost you only the registered mail fee.

We believe that when you join hands with us, Comelec will know that it's not only the #TNTrio who are doing their job but also the millions of voters who have been disenfranchised.

We encourage you to send your personal letter and this is not asking much from you as this is for our benefit and for the benefit of our country.

At our end, we will proceed with our letter to the Comelec Advisory Council as well as the Joint Congressional Oversight Committee to get copies of the Comelec reports and check if indeed their report contains the transmission data.

Our relentless effort will not stop us from from making our requests with Comelec as we are preparing for the next battle with Supreme Court on the same ground.

If all else fails, then we can honestly say that this government is denying us our sovereign right to vote and to have our vote be counted.

When that happens, then we leave this urgent matter to the Filipino voters to decide what they want to do to get the Comelec and the Supreme Court to grant our request.

Let's all pray for Comelec enlightenment so they can redeem their trust from the Filipino voters .

oooooo

3
Update – Aug. 18, 2022, 8AM
Share a Letter from one, Leo Paras

With the permission of one of our #truthwarriors, we are sharing his letter which he posted on his fb.

We are proud of your commitment to join us in these trying hours after we initially failed to get the right response from Comelec.

By Monday, we will be following up with another letter to right the wrong answer by comelec. But we will also send our request to Comelec Advisory Council and Joint Congressional Oversight Cmte on Automated Election to share with us the forwarding letter by Comelec.

This stalling gimmick is not working for Comelec. Their initial answer puts them into a spot where they don't know where their responsibility starts and when it ends.

It would have been easier if Comelec answered by claiming they have the data logs and they can provide the CDRs to us to remove any doubt about the early transmission of ERs from vcm to transparency server.

When we followed your suggestion that the #truthwarriors write their own letters with the same objective and provided you with sample letter, we received positive responses.

Together, our strength in numbers may change the dynamic of ferreting out the truth from Comelec.

This ping pong diplomacy has to end with the truth. That's our simple call and comelec who are expert lawyers couldn't even give a direct answer.

Normally, from a corporate investigation, we ask the department to submit a report on the process and that department should be the IT dept. Then the IT dept submits a thorough report about the log data and after verification, the corporate counsel will decide to submit to the President who will consult his board and secure its approval. Then and only then will the corporation issue its response.

Did the Comelec follow this kind of process at all?

We doubt it. Why? This is a simple process of ignoring a simple voter's request and they cannot even get their hands on this.

If we swamp them with thousands of letters asking for the same request, how will they handle this ? Refer them again to CAC and JCOAE?

This is a circus that is reserved for clowns. And Comelec lawyers are no clowns and they have the power to give direct answers like a simple letter request from us.

Let's pray that the power of truth overcomes their power not to tell the truth.

THE COMMISSIONERS OF ELECTION
COMMISSION ON ELECTION
Palacio del Gobernador Bldg.
Gen Luna St., Intramuros, Manila

August 18, 2022

Re: Request for proof of Transmission of Election Returns from the Vote Counting Machines for the Transparency Server

Honorable Commissioners,

I am signing this letter because I, a registered voter of Barangay San Isidro, Taytay, Rizal and a Filipino Citizen, cannot accept the result of May 9, 2022 election.

I believe the May 9 election was tainted with possible irregularities as I was not able to witness the manual count of my vote after the closing of precincts.

I could not also believe that the transmission of election returns at the very first hour is possible because there are Comelec rules on the process of ER preparation prior to transmission of the ERs from the vote counting machines to the transparency server.

Furthermore, I need to see proof of transmission such CDRs or call detail reports from the telcos which handled the transmission.

Without these presented to me for my acceptance, I cannot accept the results of the May 9 election.

I am writing this letter to express my sovereign right to know whether my vote was counted. This is expressly provided in the right of suffrage guaranteed by the 1987 Philippine Constitution (Article V. Suffrage. Sec. 1) and the sanctity of the ballot (Sec. 2) and the right of the people for redress of grievances (Bill of Rights, Sec. 4) and the right of the people on matters of public concern.

In view thereof, I hereby request that Comelec respect and not subvert the will of the people and any delay on your part in granting this request is considered in violation of the aforementioned law.

Very truly yours,

LEO A. PARAS
Precinct No. 0245A
Barangay San Isidro, Taytay, Rizal

OOOOOO

4
Update - Aug. 19, 2022, 8AM
Two Months Already

It will be two months already since this incumbent assumed his office.

Already we are witnessing topsy-turvy handling or mishandling of governance. Let's start with non-completion of his cabinet organization. Without a full working cabinet, how could you run an office efficiently and effectively ?

Some of the appointees are recycled officials from the former president and some of whom have pending cases with the office they are assigned to.

The inside stuff shows the infighting amongst the financial backers who are now claiming division of the spoils of victory. No wonder, there have been questionable appointments and even the trolls are now being rehired to attack appointees from the other camp.

The attacks have now shifted in the corridors of power and they are getting dirtier and uglier. Don't be surprised that since the focus of this incumbent is how to satisfy his supporters, who is the going to emerge the winner from this bullfight?

One of my political friends commented that after any war, history reveals the victors turn to each other and cut each other's throat. Like any power play games, it's all about the power of the purse. Whoever controls the monies, controls the economy.

What's fueling the releases of the scandals in Deped, DOH and other government agencies is the incumbent's allies want to pin the blame on the former regime and to get back the corrupted funds.

War, as perceived by one political analyst, is brewing and getting to be dominating the political scene and nobody is minding the business of governing anymore.

The victims from this fight of gladiators are the ordinary workers and businesses who are still reeling from the high inflation, rising interest rates, high gasoline prices,rising unemployment, climbing food prices, more importation of basic commodities, higher trade deficits, uncontrolled forex depreciation, hoarding of the same commodities, growing health issues with Covid comeback and new disease called monkey pox.

His economic managers can be faulted for not being forthright about addressing these economic emergencies. But this lack of good governance traces back to the highest official who is not schooled in business management at all.

I had only 6 units of economics in college and took up subjects related to finance when I pursued my MBA at Ateneo de Manila. But I only learned to appreciate economic matters when I joined Citibank treasury department. As trader, you have to weigh all economic theories, and economic activities from political angle. In the process, you are expected to decide the impact of all these factors on interest and forex rates and you make projections where these are heading.

When I started teaching treasury subject in schools, I begin my lecture with introduction of economic tools as they are the bases of how to manage liquidity and forex positions. You can make wrong decisions when you fail to analyze the impact of these economic movements.

Hence, from the political front, if the incumbent cannot handle the economic trauma from mismanagement, then you will witness spiraling of worst economic disasters.

We can only pray that when you can't handle the economy wisely, then by all means give up the reins in favor of good, tested and uncorrupted economic team.

Meanwhile, we cannot also give up our truth campaign as any truth we will unearth can change the political arena.   ooooo

5
Update - Aug. 19, 2022, 9M
Comelec Evasive Letter

As we weigh in on the evasive answer by Comelec to our July 15 letter by passing our letter to the Comelec Advisory Council (CAC) and Joint Congressional Oversight Cmte on Automated Election(JCOCAE), we will send our follow letter to Comelec this coming Monday insisting on our position that they respond truthfully and faithfully as they have the mandate to tell us the truth.

Any evasive response we will receive from them will reveal that this constitutional body is remiss and is negligent and is fully accountable and is exposing itself to possible civil and criminal case according to one lawyer.

Evasive answers can mean the accountable body is committing a cover up of the possible crime where they didn't follow their own guidelines on the election process and the serious deflection that there were logs of data where ERs were indeed transmitted from vcm to transparency server.

According to one lawyer, we don't have a case right now but if the accountable body still refuses to answer directly our request, then we can file before the SC for mandamus. If they still refuse to give us the answer, then we can file a separate case against the officials of comelec for betrayal of public trust.

This lawyer advises us that we don't need prima facing evidence as we are not filing an election protest.

My take is this. Coming from my banking experience, a similar situation exists when the bank commits major computer breakdown resulting in loss of depositors' funds . Remember the complaint by depositors against big banks who were accused of committing acts where their funds were illegally transferred or totally deleted from their account. This is the same situation where the people's votes were not counted by the accountable body and the people are demanding that they want to see the ballot boxes be opened and that their votes be counted.

Going back to banks who may be guilty of a possible inside job where bank employees and officers are guilty of illegal activities appropriating funds for themselves, the bank management will immediately announce to the public that they are investigating on their own such possible illegal act. But they will never admit the truth about the inside job. They will protect their bank by covering up said illegal act. They will fire said employees or officers and may restore missing funds but this may not be forthcoming.

Let me give you examples of inside job in banks. The IT personnel who have access to computer passwords can easily make illegal transfers. They will run after dormant accounts where there are no movements for several months. They can alter computation of interest rates like any program and siphon interest amounts to a sundry account which they can withdraw and transfer to their own account. I personally know these illegal acts because these happened in banks where I was connected before. There are more items which I can cite here but I can share these when I discuss my lecture on how banks are guilty of all kinds of scams. I published and lectured this in my subject called "Lessons from bank and investment and IT scams " which include pyramiding and money laundering .

What about the accountable body possible cover up? There is no law that should stop nor prevent this body from revealing the log data to the public because that is the mandate given to them under the election law where they are supposed to conduct election in a fair, honest, transparent and credible election to ensure the people's will and right to vote and their right for their vote to be counted. This body cannot subvert that sovereign right by not telling the truth about the election process.

We will consult further with our lawyers if the accountable body refuses to answer our request. If any case may arise from these non direct answer, then these officials have to answer before proper courts why they should not be prosecuted for their possible cover up.

If there is any good coming from our persistence or insistence on our actions including the letters you will be sending to them, we will probably see a whistleblower to come out who may not want to be accused and prosecuted.

When I was still connected with a bank as President, when a case like malversation happens with a staff suspected of committing such crime, I simply tell said staff to return the funds and if he refuses we will file a qualified theft case against the staff and qualified theft with amount over P500,000 is non bailable. Then we report to BSP the case as required by BSP and said staff will be lacklisted from bank employment. If he returns the funds, he will have to resign and we will withhold clearance from his separation as there may still be additional malversations he may have committed.

Hence, these parallel crimes from banks and the election accountable body are not remote. While the bank management can be guilty of possible cover up of the inside job, the accountable election body can also be guilty of possible cover up of an inside job.

Our pursuit of truth continues .

oooooo

6
Update, Aug. 23, 2022
Cabinet members

The other day, in a gathering of former colegio colleagues, we were mentioned #TNTrio just take it slow in our movement because we are forming good incumbent cabinets. They are speculating that they are experts in their position and most of them are from the top university UP and mentioned Finance, DTI, BSP, NEDA, DOJ. Just joking because we are the same frat men in UP and I am a member of the law frat, Alpha Phi Beta, the regime of San Beda Frats Lex Taliones is over.

During the time of dictator who was a member of Upsilon Sigma Phi of UP, he appointed many of his brothers.

It was Cory's time, relatives Inc.

During the time of FVR, the military.

During the time of Erap and GMA... just a joke both remove and jail.

PNoy's time, Ateneo connection and classmates.

Digs era, Davao connection and San Beda bros and some of his bros got imprisoned.

So, my question is, who is the connection of SD? Back to UP boys? But he didn't graduate and there's no association in the fraternity !

It's true, they are UP, where did the DSWD Sec come from?

So, back UP mafia like his dictator father?

So I'm told, Maybe we can be #TNTrio in the cabinet because Eli Rio is former DICT Usec and Gus Lagman is former Comelec commissioner.

And I was told, if you can't lick em, join em!

I told you that was a long time ago! We are invited to serve the government and as for me, I will never be in the government. Retired banker and IT is enough for me and I don't like what he said that if you can't lick em join em.

To tell the truth, I was also broken there. I came from a big multinational bank, my colleagues and boss are great. The Mafia in the group there needs to graduate top of the class of top universities here and they prefer those who have masters in prestigious business schools in America like Wharton, Harvard .

So, how did I get to be among those graduates who were not despised by UP Foreign Service and did MBA in Ateneo while being an employee of Citibank. The bank has a program that if you study masters while you are an employee, their answer is tuition on pro rata basis. If your grade is A, 100 pct reimbursement, B 75 pct, C, 50 pct. I won't say my grades anymore, it's embarrassing because the background of foreign service in business is far.

But, I can say that I persevered as a clerk in the loans and securities department. But I studied my job and submitted suggestions on how to improve your work because there is a suggestion award given by Citibank. I had a lot of awards before and maybe I was recognized there as having the potential to be an official.

But my chance to be accepted in the executive program is far because they are all graduates abroad.

When there was an opening in the treasury department, I applied and there I was trained by those who are good in the treasury and succeeded.

Citibank has a policy to collect the rank and file of candidates for the executive development program. And I was recommended by my treasury boss and I was accepted among the famous graduates.

For one year training, I studied operations and learned the controls of banking. I will memorize the rules and regulations because there is an exam in every department. It didn't take me one year because I'm already from operations when I was a clerk. Six months and I was promoted and they put me as an account officer in the financial institutions department.

It didn't take long, I was sent to the America Head Office of Citibank and I was trained in credit.

My colleagues are really good in training from branches all over the world. Very happy because the trainers and my fellow trainees are really good.

When I come back, I will be promoted because I developed a lot of products and earned a lot from the bank.

It didn't take long before the head in New York made an offer and hired me to be the head of Asia Pacific financial institutions dept. But my local boss didn't pass me and I didn't endorse.

I felt bad and when there was a big offer in the local banks, I decided to move.

After that, the foreign service graduate was so despicable until he became the president of a local bank.

So what can I say to my colleagues that there is a mafia inside Malaccanyang that are from UP.

We are #TNTrio even though we are from UP, we are not included in the mafia because our wish is to know the truth. We are seniors now and we don't have time to join the mafia, any mafia.

What a person who is seated should do and have the right vetting process and not betting process.

Who brought down the Philippines isn't it a law graduate of UP who became a dictator.

So Not true that whether you are from UP or high finish is important in choosing cabinet .

My FB is just here, Others said that if we win in our dreams, we should be in the government.

We do not wish to join anyone's administration. We are done and we are retired and we will just raise our grandchildren and the youth should be the ones who serve in the government.

Our time has ended. And our golden lesson to the youth is study well and don't join the mafia especially the bad mafia.

If you remember the Erap jokes: "Tell me who your friends are... ::" Erap said " and I will tell you mine . "

So don't join devils camp and soon you will be one of them.

(In Filipino)

Nung isang araw po, sa isang pagtitipon ng mga dating kasamahan sa colegio, nabanggit na kami daw #TNTrio maghinay hinay lang sa kilusan namin kasi nabubuo naman daw na mahuhusay na kabinete ng incumbent. Tinutukoy po nila na mga dalubhasa naman daw sa kanilang position at karamihan ay galing sa top university UP at binanggit Yung Finance, DTI, BSP, NEDA, DOJ. Sa pagbibiro kasi pare pareho kami frat men sa UP at ako kasapi ng law frat, Alpha Phi Beta, tapos na daw ang regimen ng mga San Beda Frat Lex Taliones.

Nung panahon ni diktador na kasapi ng Upsilon Sigma Phi ng UP, Marami siya inappoint mga brods niya.

Nung panahon naman daw ni Cory mga kamaganak Inc.

Nung panahon ni FVR mga militar.

Nung panahon ni Erap at GMA…biro lang pareho tanggal at kulong.

Panahon ni Pnoy, Ateneo connection at klasmates.

Panahon ni Digs, Davao connection at San Beda brods at nakulong pa ilang brods niya .

So, Tanung ko, sino naman connection ni SD? Balik UP boys ? Pero Hindi naman nag tapos siya at wala naman association sa fraternity !

Totoo, mga UP nga eh Saan naman Galing Yung DSWD Sec?

So, balik UP mafia katulad ng Tatay niyang diktador ?

Kaya Sabi sa akin, Baka Pwede kami #TNTrio sa kabinete dahil si Eli Rio ay dating DICT Usec at si Gus Lagman ay dating Comelec commissioner.

At Sabi pa sa akin, if you can't lick em, join em!

Sabi ko naman matagal na yan ! Imbita kami to serve the government at ako po Wala ako sa gobyerno kahit Kailan . Retired banker na lng at IT Tama na sa akin yan at Ayoko Yang sinabi niya na if you can't lick em join em.

Sa totoo lang, nasira na rin po ako Jan. Galing po ako sa malaking multinational bank, mahuhusay po mga kasama at boss ko. Ang Mafia naman po sa group doon ay Kailangan graduate ka top of the class ng top universities dito at preferred nila mga May masters sa prestigious business schools sa America katulad ng Wharton, Harvard .

So, Papano naman ako nakasama sa mga graduates na yan ay Di hamak ng UP Foreign Service lang po at nag MBA sa Ateneo habang empleyado ng Citibank. May program po ang Bangko na pag nag aral ka ng masters habang empleyado ka, sagot nila tuition on pro rata basis. Pag A ang grade mo 100 pct reimbursement, B 75 pct, C, 50 pct . Hindi ko na sabihin ang grades ko po nakakhiya kasi malayo background ng foreign service sa business.

Pero, masasabi ko po nag tiyaga po bilang isang clerk sa loans and securities dept Pero inaral ko trabaho ko at submit ako suggestions on how to improve your work Kasi Meron suggestion award po bigay Citibank . Dami ko awards po noon at doon ako siguro nakilala bilang May potential na maging opisyal din.

Pero malayo chance ko matanggap sa executive program kasi puro nga mga graduates abroad .

Nang May opening sa treasury dept nag apply po ako at doon Na train ako ng mga magagaling sa treasury at umasenso naman.

May policy po ang Citibank na kumukuha sa rank and file ng candidate para sa executive development program . At Na recommend ako ng treasury boss ko at natanggap ako kabilang sa mga sikat ng graduates.

For one year training, inaral ko po operations at inalam ko mga controls ng banking . Memorize ko po rules and regulations kasi May examen bawat dept. Hindi po ako Inabot ng one year kasi Galing na ako sa operations nung clerk ako. Six months at na promote ba po ako at nalagay nilang account officer sa financial institutions dept.

Hindi nagtagal, pinadala po ako sa America Head Office ng Citibank at pinag training pa ako sa credit .

Mahuhusay po talaga mag kasama ko sa training na Galing sa mga branches sa buong mundo. Tuwang tuwa po kasi magagaling po talaga ang mga trainors at mga Kapwa trainees ko po.

Pagbalik ko po promoted ako dahil Marami ako na develop products at Kumita ng malaki ang Bangko.

Hindi nag tagal nag offer ang head sa New York at kinukuha ako para maging head ng Asia pacific financial institutions dept . Pero Hindi ako pinanasin ng local boss ko at Hindi ako endorse.

Sumama loob ko at nung May malaking offer sa mga local banks nag decision na ako na lumipat.

After that, taas noo pa ang hamak ng foreign service graduate hanggang sa naging president ng isang local bank.

Kaya Ano masasabi ko sa mga kasamahan ko na May mafia daw sa loob ng Malakanyang na mga taga UP.

Kami po #TNTrio kahit mga taga UP po kami, Hindi po kami kasama sa mafia kasi ang hangarin po namin ay malaman ang katotohanan . Seniors na po kami at Wala kaming panahon sumali sa mga mafia kahit anong mafia.

Ang Dapat Gawin ng isang nakaupo at mag ka roon ng Tamang vetting process at hindi bettting process po.

Sino po nag pabagsak ng Pilipinas ay Di ba law graduate ng UP na naging diktador.

Kaya Hindi totoo na kung Galing ka sa UP o mataas na tinapusan ay mahalaga sa pagpili ng kabinete

Dito Ing po fb ko, Sabi ng Iba pag tayo nagwagi sa hangarin natin Dapat na sa gobyerno kami.

Hindi po kami nag hahangad sumali kahit kaninong administration. Tapos na po kami at retirado na po kami at magpapalaki na lang po kami ng mga apo namin at Dapat mga kabataan naman ang mag silbi sa gobyerno.

Tapos na panahon po namin. At ang Gintong aral po namin sa mga kabataan mag aral po kayo maigi at huwag sumali sa mafia lalo na Yung masamang mafia .

Kung natatandaan po niyo mga Erap jokes: "Tell me who your friends are…::" Sabi ni Erap " and I will tell you mine ."

So don't join devils camp and soon you will be one of them.

oooooo

7
Update, Aug. 25, 2022 –
Support Petition

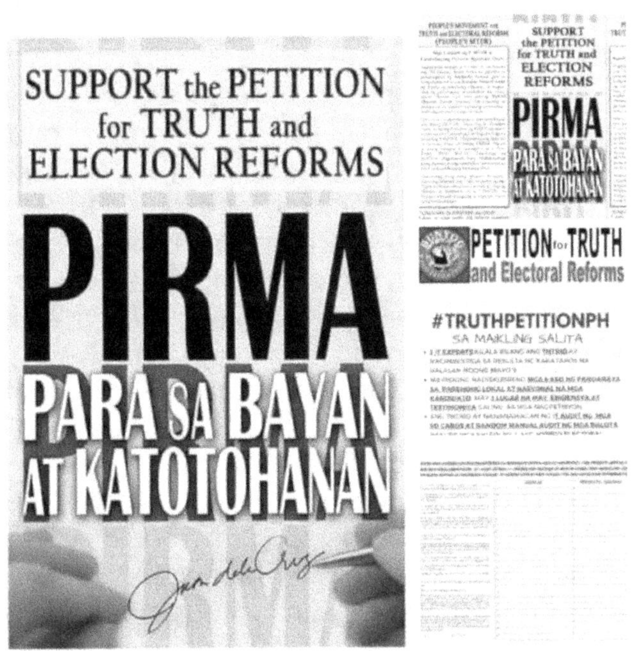

Support and sign the nationwide signature campaign on Monday, August 29,2022 sa Araw ng mga Bayani.

Petition to demand transparency from COMELEC for the rampant rigging of the automated electoral process and evidence of irregularities as well as to demand a hybrid electoral system:

• Manual System: Voting and counting of ballots in polling precincts

• Automated System: Transmission of Votes to the National Server and Canvassing of Votes.

oooooo

8
Update, Aug. 28, 2022
Need for Prayer

A prayer for election truth?

A #truthwarrior asked me if I can compose a prayer for election truth.

I have not composed an election prayer and the usual prayers we recite are available in prayer books.

In fact, there are so many prayers for truth but I have not encountered a prayer for election truth . There are prayers announced by Church ministers or priests but these prayers are recited before an election .

The prayer being requested is a prayer after election fraud has allegedly been committed.

So how do we write a prayer for election truth ?

I have been seeking intercession from our saints, our very own Blessed Mother, her Son, and the Holy Trinity and invoking their divine intervention to help us unearth the truth behind the alleged irregularities.

Since we the #TNTrio began our campaign for truth, we were met initially with lackadaisical support. We were even advised to drop our solicitation and discontinue our messaging of our appeals for the regulatory bodies to respond to our requests . Thus far, we have not been successful in getting direct answers from the election body.

Just take the case of the 120k Pangasinan voters who were denied twice by the Comelec for their request to open the ballot boxes and count manually the ballots cast there. They are in their last mile of appeal and this time they will be filing before the Supreme Court citing the sovereign rights of the voters.

We are clutching at straws according to some legal pundits as we don't have prima facie evidence to prove there's massive cheating.

But let's break down our appeal.

Our appeal hinges on the possible irregularities when we simulated the election process.

As IT experts, we were following the automated election process and while conducting the simulated election process, there were questions we raised and we wanted to get hold of copies of documents which will prove the conduct of the election was above board.

The closest we are now getting to prove that there doubtful processes which were provided by the election process and we are simply asking for proof whether there was transmission made during the first hour after the election closed at 7. We cannot get hold of the CDRs or call detail reports from the telcos because it's oniy the comelec which has exclusive right on these CDRs as they are the subscribers of these telcos. Getting a court order, as suggested by some lawyers, is one of the options for us so we can get the copies of the CDRs.

As citizens and registered voters, we insisted in our letters to the Comelec that we have the right to know these CDRs so once they disclose these to us, then we can end our search for truth.

In our presentations to the Comelec and to the Comelec Advisory Council and the Joint Congressional Oversight cmte on automated election, we narrated our observations that it's impossible to transmit the 20M votes in one hour from the vcm to the transparency server. This has to be proven or disproven by the Comelec and we need such proof.

So how do we compose the election truth prayer?

Perhaps we can invite some of our #truthwarriors to send us their suggestions and then we can compose a significant prayer for all.

The prayer must be short and must bear our indulgence and forbearance as we do not want to incite any attempt to attack person or persons so we can get the proper attention from the Comelec.

I still subscribe to the tenets of the author, Sun Tzu of the Art of War and connect these to the power of the

Almighty. Sun Tzu is an advocate for non violence as this is his definition of the Art of War. Google him and his book and let's see how we can win the minds of Comelec to our side.

oooooo

9
Update, Aug. 28, 2022 –
Truth Warrior Prayer

I will attempt to write this truth election prayer but i will call this #truthwarriorprayer. A thanksgiving prayer.

Dear Lord,
Thank you for for choosing us #truthwarriors to fight for the truth.

Thank you for enlightening us #truthwarriors that there is hope in our petition.

Thank you for giving us #truthwarriors the strength to continue with our advocacy till the truth comes out.

Thank you for believing in the millions of us #truthwarriors who will give you back the faith we have failed and lost in our country.

Thank you for that special day when we #truthwarriors will once again become your faithful children as you vanquish the evil forces who displease you.

Amen.

oooooo

10
Update – Aug. 29, 2022
Forensic Science

To our followers, we, #TNTrio are now close to our forensic investigation of the election fraud.

If we follow the logical mind of Sherlock Holmes, the famous detective character created by Sir Arthur Conan Doyle, we are not far behind in our attempt to solve the election crime.

This is the inductive reasoning of Sherlock Holmes:

"From the scene of the crime, he uses his observations skills, then establishes patterns, then draws his hypothesis and concludes with his theory."

Sir Arthur Conan Doyle, author of this character Sherlock Holmes, has long been credited as an influence to forensic science due to his character's use of methods such as fingerprints, serology, ciphers, trace evidence and footprints long before they were commonly used by police forces.

Let me add to this famous author before we get distracted by alluding to Sherlock Holmes stories to solve election crime .

What we can learn from inductive reasoning which Sherlock Holmes employs, is his principle of discovery :

"He starts off with his observations, writes down the facts, then establishes patterns, then attempts to prove his hypothesis and finally draws his theory."

But more importantly, before and after he visits the crime scene, he never stops to question and asks WHY every step of the way.

You can go ahead and read Sherlock Holmes stories as they are entertaining and stories of logical reasoning. These books are a must reading from my HS years. But in UP, from my philosophy subject, I recommend you read the book of Copi et al, Introduction to Logic, as this has a bearing on what we#TNTrio are exactly doing and have done so far:

If you have been following us, we will give you fair results of our investigation of the election fraud:

"We started off with our observations from the night of election crime, then listed the facts, then drew the patterns, traced the beginning of how the crime evolved, then put up our hypothesis and the final theory ." What's missing is the hard evidence of transmission data or CDRs which will complete our investigation.

If you will recall, our hardworking and super efficient sleuth, former DICT Eli Rio already drew the patterns of electronic manipulation of how the results were released in the first hour. He traced back to the same from the socmed false propaganda, to fake surveys to the final manipulation of automated election system.

Through our letters to Comelec, we sought disclosure of this transmission data which is number one evidence to finally prove our hypothesis and theory.

If we fail to secure this, then we proceed to the Supreme Court until we are able to secure this evidence.

Pray that our sleuthing efforts will not fail our search for the truth behind the election crime.

5:43

...coach.substack.com

British writer Sir Arthur Conan Doyle created the character Sherlock Holmes to become the best detective in the world by seeing the none obvious at every crime scene. Unlike fictional superheroes, Doyle did not equip Holmes with specialized capabilities—only the power of induction. We all need to form a process of our own when observing situations using the power of inductive reasoning. We need to ask why more often. We need to stop jumping to false conclusions, then collecting the data which will support our decisions.

We all cannot think like Sherlock Holmes. Still, we can endeavor to use inductive reasoning to help us with our daily decision making.

Please forward and share this email with your friends and family.

♡ 13

6:12

🔒 books.google.com.ph

← Google Books   GET BOOK

Introduction to

LOGIC

Irving M. Copi
Carl Cohen
Victor Rodych

15th edition

5:43

...coach.substack.com

COACH The Daily Coach

> **Deduction:** *Theory to Hypothesis to Observatio to Confirmation*
>
> **Induction:** *Observation to Pattern to Hypothesi Theory*

In this case, Sherlock Holmes used inductive reasoning. He observed the scene, noticed certa jewelry on the woman's body had been recently cleaned, except for her wedding ring. That forc him to ask the question, *Why*? Why would she clean everything except her wedding ring? Holı induced that the woman did not commit suicid In part, because she was traveling to London fo one day, she packed an overnight bag—and had secret meeting before returning home. The secı meeting and wedding ring, all allowed Holmes continue to probe the none obvious, asking questions along the way but never forming a fir opinion. Sherlock Holmes behaves like an annoying child who continually asks, *Why*. The "*whys*" stack upon one another, and before too long, they allow Holmes to form a pattern to re: a hypothesis and then a final theory.

5:43

...coach.substack.com

British writer Sir Arthur Conan Doyle created the character Sherlock Holmes to become the best detective in the world by seeing the none obvious at every crime scene. Unlike fictional superheroes, Doyle did not equip Holmes with specialized capabilities—only the power of induction. We all need to form a process of our own when observing situations using the power of inductive reasoning. We need to ask why more often. We need to stop jumping to false conclusions, then collecting the data which will support our decisions.

We all cannot think like Sherlock Holmes. Still, we can endeavor to use inductive reasoning to help us with our daily decision making.

Please forward and share this email with your friends and family.

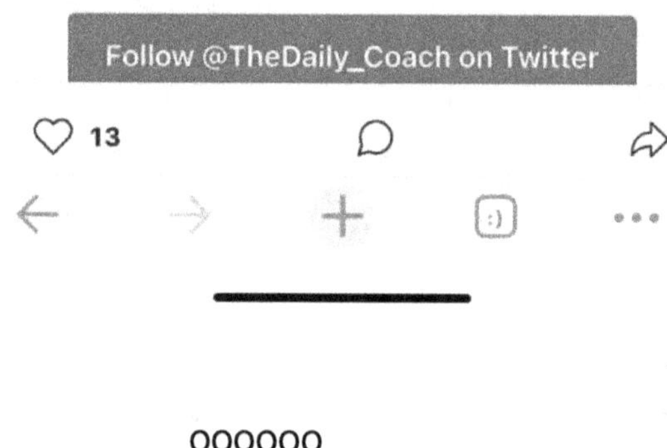

OOOOOO

11
Update, Aug. 31, 2022
Student Election System

Let me share what I presented to a business group early on after the May 9 election my observation. Take note that unlike the comparative presentation of a simple system which I develop for banks, the simple automated election system by smartmatic and implemented by comelec does not contain the minimum basic requirements which my bank clients require from a solution provider like my company.

While turnover of a system between my bank clients and my company is confidential, the turnover of smartmatic to comelec which acquired the automated election system is not properly disclosed to the voting public.

Why is there a wall between a government body which administers automated election and the voting public which requires transparency in the conduct of election?

If Comelec bought the system and the source code from smartmatic, what's the price of the system? Was there public bidding as required by law?

In my org, we conducted the same simple election process which was provided by a local school whose student programmers designed exactly the same system with full description of features of the system. This automated election system is being used by schools in their election of student council officers. We just lease the equipment and we have our own comelec which observes the process . Our voters are the equivalent of one precinct and it took the operator less than an hour to process the 700 votes . So how come our each vcm can process 20M votes in just an hour ?

The student group who provided us their own product costs much less than the P10B comelec paid smartmatic. In fact, we just lease the equipment and we provided them the list of candidates which are printed in the ballot and the marking on the ballot is by shading the small circle in front of the name of the candidate. After election, the system also produces an election return. After this, we conduct random manual checking. The machine also has an operating sd card which contains the names of the qualified voters and it has a program to read the shaded boxes and count the number of votes cast per candidate .

In the future elections, why don't we patronize our own student programmers and provide them with funds to build the vcm?

So who is claiming that the smartmatic is the best automated system provided by this Venezuela company which incidentally is now the subject of investigation in the recently concluded election in Kenya.

Let's take a big look at this automated election system developed by our very own Filipino programmers.

To be frank, we just rent the unit and pay them professional fee and the amount is less than P100k.

If we need 26,000 vcms, it would only cost us P2.6M to rent them.

3:12   

Done **Forum June14 202…**   🔍

ooooooo

12
Update, Sep. 1, 2022
Economic Outlook

Update on economic outlook from my favorite economist, former BSP DG Diwa Guinigundo.

True. But when the illegitimate incumbent spends P87B in two months is already a measure of unbridled, unexplainable and unaccountable expenses plus budget blowout for office of OVP, we do not foresee an economic uptick.

With rising interest rates, depleting international reserves, depreciating pesos, higher imports(sugar, rice), uncontrolled borrowings, business outlook is dire and if the illegitimate incumbent continues to fiddle while economy is running loose, quo vadis Philippines ?

Investors are still on wait and see ever since he grabbed power through illegitimate means.

Some doomsday economists are predicting worse things to come .

Government debts are expected to surpass the trillion debt incurred by the diabolic president.

How does the real future of the economy look like the rest of the year ? Or the next 5 years?

Just brace yourselves for the worst. Save if you can. Do not buy or invest in real estate. Maybe buy dollars now as the peso is expected to depreciate further . Hold on to business expansion . Keep personnel to minimum. Hold credit sales as financing cost is on the rise. Avoid imports as volatile exchange rates can push up cost further without recovery from add on prices and market resistance. Do not splurge or plunge into buying unnecessary items.

In short, economy may either be on a standstill or may be spinning downward.

How do we hedge against this backdrop of economic meltdown ?

Definitely, we cannot stop the train of unwarranted expenses by the illegitimate incumbent but we can join our movement to upend the cheating smartmatic and support our comelec and Supreme Court petitions.

Too bad. God knows he didn't win and we are left in the dark and we are now suffering or going deep into quagmire from disastrous impact of bad governance by the illegitimate incumbent.

But it's not too late. Support our pirmahan for truth and pray to God to spare us from the harm of further mismanagement by the illegitimate incumbent.

Article of Diwa Guinigundo which appeared Manila Bulletin today:

All up, we might be seeing sustained increases in market interest rates, weaker peso, and perhaps higher business taxes. Growth could reach a respectable growth rate of around 6.5 percent because it is difficult to forecast higher consumption and business activities due to rapid inflation and external uncertainty. With more competent and upright governance, the likelihood of sound economic growth is stronger.

oooooo

13
Update - Sep. 1, 2022, 2PM
Slow Progress

It's September 2, Friday, and I have been getting feedback from many of you #truthwarriors.

I made several predictions already regarding economic forecast but as I said I am no economist but just a retired banker and IT person.

A word of advice to #truthwarriors.

Study with a grain of salt my posts and they are not meant to encourage you to take drastic actions. My economic posts are meant to give you big picture of our economy and we cannot go out into the streets and protest right away.

As I mentioned here in my several posts, we want to clear our way to the truth by following legal processes. Otherwise, we lose our battle for truth.

Per our lawyers advice, we need to follow the rules even as they study ways how to even out our battle for the truth against the apparent disregard by regulatory bodies re our requests.

We are on the finishing stages of our effort and we will keep you posted of our moves.

So far, we are getting closer to the truth and the evidence we want will prove we are on the right side of the truth.

Our lawyers want to prove an airtight case before the Supreme Court and won't let any stone left unturned and make the Supreme court respect the people's genuine will as provided by the election law.

If the Supreme court will not uphold our sovereign right to know the truth by opening ballot boxes and manually counting the ballots and by giving us the transmission data to prove that there were transmissions made in the first hour of 20M votes, then we will let you know .

Then and only then we will let you decide on what actions you may want to take to redress our grievances as this is also allowed under our constitution.

Didn't I always remind you about what the former Speaker Amang Rodrigues said about success " slow by slow we will success."

The economic outlook may not be good under this illegitimate incumbent but I also advised everyone to make adjustments for the meantime.

Let's see what happens in the coming days or weeks or months but definitely not years as we expect our campaign for truth to end soon with the blessing of the Lord of Truth.

oooooo

14
Update - Sep. 1, 2022 6PM
Art of War by Sun Tzu

I keep mentioning this book, the Art of War, by a Chinese military a strategist and philosopher Sun Tzu.

This book which I understand is a required reading for military schools in US and in the Philippines is both an interesting and helpful book in making strategies when you face conflict in war or in our personal and business life.

If you follow this philosophy or tenets of Sun Tzu, you will win any war or conflict without shedding blood.

As for me, I have been influenced by this philosopher and his philosophy has helped me overcome my weaknesses and has strengthened my resolve to move forward and face my adversaries both in my personal and in my business life.

The book is self explanatory and you will find wisdom from this philosopher.

In our truth campaign we are also guided by the same philosophy and if you might have noticed, we can put our adversaries on the defensive where they may have little option except to surrender to our demand.

Just remember the art of war is not the art of deception which our adversaries employ and in due time, they will realize they are defeated even before they try to deflect us into submission .

Still the most powerful weapon we have is our unceasing prayers to the Almighty who can vanquish the lies and the liars and raise the army of truth warriors .

oooooo

15
Update, Sep. 2, 2022, 7AM
Forex Rate Predictions

I hate making predictions about forex rate.

Yesterday, Ist day of September, dollar closed at P56.61.

Today, September 2, the dollar closed at P56.81.

If political instability rules, just how far will the dollar move before it hits P60.00. You are right in just one month or by the end of September, all prices will jump around 20 pct, from gas to commodities which are import pegged.

Right now, my clients are worried that if this rate goes up any further, then it would be very expensive to import. But for those who want to pursue their business even if the forex rates are highly volatile, they will price themselves out of the market, meaning consumers will just stop buying or postpone expenditures.

I can't predict the end game of this forex game. My fiends in the parallel market are making hay as they can cut as much as P0.05 to P0.10 per dollar.

To those clients who fear the forex will go haywire, some banks may offer forward rates, meaning they can lock in the rates over a period of time but they have to pay a premium.

Meanwhile, what happens to Juan de la Cruz?

Yes. I am like you guys and when I buy my food needs from the nearby supermarket, a budget of P500 per can't meet the meals for a family of 5. What about the transport ? Already there are clamor from public transport increasing utility rates.

Some of us are also demanding higher minimum wage.

This will go on and on as market will not subside with unstable political leadership .

How and what can we expect when these illegitimately elected leaders want to print more monies to fund their 2023 budget. Instead of controlling inflationary effects of the rise of forex, interest rates, they don't care at all.

Just like the diabolic leadership of the previous administration where corruption led to printing of up to P13T debt, they have already spent P87B in just two months.

Let's face it. We can't absorb the negative impact of this unbridled and bloated budget where revenues are hardly expected. If businesses are down, who's gonna pay those corporate taxes? If imports go down, so will customs taxes ?

So what do we do?

My pension is not enough to meet my daily needs. My children are already well placed in US but they too are paying mortgages for their housing, education of their children.

Senior citizens are facing the brunt too.

I feel safe as the local government subsidizes my monthly medicine requirements which otherwise would have cost me P2k per month.

What about families who do not get subsidies as many are still out of work .

The Ayuda by DSWD and LGU May soon run out if budget is exhausted.

Now, for your emergency and medical attention from public hospitals, there are huge budget cuts. They just cut PGH budget .

How about education ? They just slashed budget of UP and while tuition is free for college students, would UP survive in meeting faculty salaries etc?

This illegitimate incumbent doesn't mind cutting all these necessary budget for health and education, while they gallop with glee padding their budgets at the expense of the public needs.

Under this dire and threatening economic scenarios, the people may soon rise against the extravagant government. History is not kind to these people who make their constituents suffer as the people will at one time rise up against them.

Beware and be wary if the illegitimate incumbent continues its revelry and pads its pockets at the expense of the poor masses. The tide may turn against them.

oooooo

16
Update – Sept. 3, 2022
Directory

TRUTH PETITION PH
Coordinator Directory for Manual Written Signatures
(Assisted by Bunyog Partylist)
https://bit.ly/TruthPetitionDirectory

As of August 5, 2022, 7:52 PM

MAIN:
Bunyog Pagkakaisa Party
NATIONAL HEADQUARTERS
#3048 Lot 5 Lazaro Compound F. Bautista St.
Ugong, Valenzuela City
Landline: (02) 82510586
0935-0866363
0947-8371796

ROBERT "CULEX" SOLIMAN
National Secretary-General

PLACE	NAME / MESSENGER NAME	CONTACT NUMBER
LUZON		
NCR – National Capital Region		
Metro Manila	Marites Tepzat / Mari Thaz	09338236198
Caloocan		
10th Avenue, Caloocan City	David Valencesino	09159904723
Bagong Silang, Caloocan City	Daisy dela Cruz Beliganio	09298964727
Camarin, Caloocan City	Sir Peter Nazarate	0963 876 3517
Malabon		
Hulong Duhat, Malabon	Onggie Ong	09455020120
Malabon	Edwin Salazara Sinagota	09693950000
Valenzuela		
Valenzuela	Jonathan Ponferrado / Angat Bulsa, Valenzuela	09254640005
Valenzuela City	Jesusita Abapcia	09692816875
Tangalan, Valenzuela	Minda Manansala	09484635626

Quezon City		
Batasan, Quezon City	Banel Alvarez	09669472773
Culiao, Quezon City	Bereguetta Sarselloo	09215747097
Holy Spirit, Quezon City	Nelia Tabbada	09178475787
North Fairview, Quezon City	Bhany Torres	09672146468
Old Balara, Quezon City	Myrna Roque	09953698346
Pasong Putik, Quezon City	Onofre Cabrera	09080860443
Project 4, QC	Chloe Ann Saldana	09420300209
Brgy. VMC, Prpj. 4, QC	Jammie B Cu	09172561487
Quezon City	Cabrera Gutierrez Onofre	09090860443
Quezon City	Juliet S Ayante	-
Quezon City	Melanie S. Bojos	09690378494
Quezon City, Metro Manila	Hermosa Sanez	09171270023
San Agustin, Novaliches, Quezon City	Patty Basilan Ugtalan	09682918342
Sta. Lucia, Novaliches, QC	Andrea Alura	09156131140
West Ave. Quezon City	Ramon Lulier	09291753932
Marikina		
Concepcion Dos, Marikina	Leonor Cajilig Libcan / Beng Cajilig Libcan	09063202364
Marikina City (Convenor, Marikina Kakampinks Coalition)	Zaldy Cornelio	09094342726
Marikina Heights, Marikina City	Atty Marina Abinsuman	09164946584
Pasig		
Maybunga, Pasig City	Joselito Sangalang	09398428149
Rosario, Pasig City	Faith Andres	09192760936
San Nicolas, Pasig	Jose Ginan Tuazon Buizan	09175163071
Taguig		
FTI, Taguig City	Angel De la Guardia	09353314287
Taguig City	Bobby Fuentes Sarmiento	09983738370

Upper Bicutan, Taguig City	Quto Alba	09619797435
Makati		
Guadalupe, Makati	Thelma Precious Chua	09399031957
Makati	Jun Begeral	0916-2391519
Makati City	Thelma Quito Danuipag	09269145701
Salcedo, Makati	Cita Del	09209200677
Manila		
Sampaloc, Manila	Judy Salpingan	09152198129
Sampaloc, Manila	Enne Cristina Sanchez	(0920)9208248
Tondo, Manila	Cristina Go / Go Carlo	0960 007 3185
Mandaluyong		
Beni, Mandaluyong City	Gargay Carpio	09165827168
Mandaluyong	Yan Cipcua	09422473242
San Juan		
San Juan	Anne Umali	09462016549
San Juan, Metro Manila	Ruby Laureta Beltran	09216434421
Mandaluyong		
Mauway, Mandaluyong City	Manuel Perez	09613089738 Landline 77182712
Parañaque		
Garcia Hts. Subdivision, Sucat, Paranaque	Velyn Adueplo	09369501110
Parañaque	Lyndon Crisostomo	09966204600
San Isidro, Parañaque	Lea Nehram	09100422687
Las Piñas		
Las Piñas	Esper Zamora	09176331799
Talon 2, Las Pinas City	Mento Gallera Aguila	09299670088
Muntinlupa		
Muntinlupa City	Annie Gillega	09070631038

Region I - Ilocos Region

Ilocos Norte		
Laoag City, Ilocos Norte	Manuel Ramiro	09213031317
Pasuquin, Ilocos Norte	Marshal Felix Josue	0921 706 7244
La Union		
Agoo / Rosario, La Union	Nomel Agoo	09635258787
Bacnotan, La Union	Mae Yerona Baddang	0917-7209365
Pangasinan		
Bautista, Pangasinan	Efren Gawel	09278841896
Mangatarem, Pangasinan	Marinela Estatillo Galicia	09215798446

Region II – Cagayan Valley

Cagayan		
Ballesteros, Cagayan	Lydia Derra Ramos	09173031271
Tuguegarao City, Cagayan	Lenia Cobbs	-
Isabela		
Santiago City, Isabela	Anne Chua	09171205784

Region III – Central Luzon

Bataan		
Bataan	Joseph Gonzales	09682601080
San Pablo, Dinalupihan, Bataan	Maryrose Snyder Ganacuanco	-
Bulacan		
Balagtas, Bulacan	Elocadina Cruz	09753633449
Bustos, Bulacan	Nelson Esteves	09391698596
Calumpit, Bulacan	Jake Austin Candido	09557022113

Calumpit, Bulacan	Rosalina Yanga	09321031746
Calumpit, Malolos, Guiginto, Bulacan	Gee Garbo Luchavez	09064205292
Citrus, City of San Jose del Monte, Bulacan	Rowena Ignacio	09976513973
District 2, City of San Jose del Monte, Bulacan	Elvie Sayosa Madriaga	09106103538
Meycauayan, Bulacan	Jimmy de Vera	09227107052
Norzagaray, Bulacan	Oh Lip	09653328153
Pajo, Meycauayan, Bulacan	Marilyn Alijano Baylon	09532444808
Sta. Maria, Bulacan	Angelie Flores	09618772322
Nueva Ecija		
Lupao, Nueva Ecija	Weng de Vera	09772004275
Pampanga		
Angeles City, Pampanga	Oliey Casala	09499899926
Arayat, Pampanga	Senaida Trajico	09053436469 / 09234490549
Bacolor, Pampanga	Connie Chan	09363616645
Lubao, Pampanga	Gracia Carisma	09190981759
Magalang, Pampanga	Leonel Lapacilao	09773992987
San Fernando, Pampanga	Enrico Dalisay Canlas	-
San Fernando, Pampanga	Bagnil Rosales Apineo	09613663219
Tarlac		
Tarlac City	Hermin Sani	09171671433
Canas, Tarlac	Elizabeth Garcia	09226244846
Zambales		
Cabangan, Zambales	Abigail Tadeo Daguyos	09273524677
Olongapo City	Jess P Bernal	09068190699
Olongapo City	Emilia Sanchez	09989763348

Region IV-A – CALABARZON

Batangas		
Agoncillo, Batangas	Zie Reyes Molinar	09199737028
Batangas City	Crisanta Samera	09069555790
Calaca, Batangas	Cora Velasco Rosales	0996 172 6913
Cuenca, Batangas	Arthur A Aguila	09989587447
Lobo, Batangas	Sam Bayan	09057982413
Padre Garcia, Batangas	Benedict Mendoza	09122814076
San Jose, Batangas	Jhun Gahinbin	09225647357
San Pascual, Batangas	Ninyo Garagas Daza	09508504568
Cavite		
Bacoor / Gen. Trias, Cavite	Imelda Balcruz / Mbel Mbel	09562955706
Cavite	Susan Cogillo	09567884818
Gen. Trias, Cavite	Jessie Garino	09914005035
Imus, Cavite	Mariya Co	09064039552
Imus, Cavite	Ric Liguit	09177088805
ICP / San Agustin, Dasmarinas City, Cavite	Rei Ella Guillet	0949 958 0211
Luzviminda 2, Dasmariñas, Cavite	Jundle Fuentes Arope	09915477951
Mendez, Cavite	Maria Liza Diza	09209114546
Noveleta, Cavite	Nini Inocancio Lumuosad	09165840804
Noveleta, Cavite	Eric John Luig	09663588003
San Marino, Salawag, Dasmariñas, Cavite	Maria Lynette Ordas Tanglao	09201283547
Silang, Cavite	Alban Adas	09369373201
Laguna		
Calauan, Laguna	Haselma Gatangal	09453501910
Calauan, Laguna	Lyn Gecana	09153056450
Calauan, Laguna	Walter Urcilla	09462814676

Los Baños, Laguna	Bolondoy Ortiga	09261680627
Pacita Complex 1, San Pedro City, Laguna	Marlyn Gernandiso / Arvin Gernandiso	0966-523-8793
San Pedro, Laguna	Cely Carnagay II	0999 417 2384
Sta. Cruz, Laguna	Manuel Canotal Bejda	09175075699
Sta. Rosa, Laguna	Annie Reyes Sarampines	09159758664
Quezon		
Atimonan, Quezon	Luis Mercado	09500928909
Lopez, Quezon Province	Denzell Kitchen	09071923272
Lucban, Quezon	Brando Ledriga	09985966935
Lucena City, Quezon Province	Jaja Matriano / Jacov Matriano	09605007752
Brgy. 10, Lucena City, Quezon Province	Anna Pren	09636813341
Balilio Island, Quezon	Geraldine Aslejada	09516192737
Quezon / Perez / Alabat Island, Quezon Province	Arlene dela Torre	09959019707
San Narciso, Quezon Province	Ramon Aureads	09461114363
Tayabas, Quezon Province	Nini Romero Gabis	09282405875
Rizal		
Angono, Rizal	Emesto Carpalig	0907 304 45 95
Antipolo City	Lydia Supicion	09296419602
Antipolo City	Maria Paz M. Tugada / Maripaz Marquez Tugada	+639454321043
Binangonan, Rizal	Luzminda Cebanico	09774653823
Binangonan, Rizal	Jayex Aubine	09555983955
Cainta, Rizal	Ling Cortez	09224024018
Cainta, Rizal	Bezza M Tan	09213467008
Midtown Village, Cainta, Rizal	Renee Galicio	09490878939
Montalban, Rizal	Aries Iv Medina	0921 4985021
Montalban, Rizal	Dong Villarin	09959613119

Morong, Rizal	Eli Garnavillas	09162434743
Morong, Rizal	Sherwin A Martin	09089439768
San Mateo, Rizal	Lucraminda Sicbun	09977731475
Muzon Taytay, Rizal	Aurora Salda	09512840935
Taytay, Rizal	Tessie Lumbao Tarnagan	09173002495
Taytay	Jenelyn Tabinga	09058368411

MIMAROPA Region

Marinduque		
Marinduque	Mauro Sol	09155387241
Occidental Mindoro		
San Jose, Occidental Mindoro	Karen Trajeca	09190999985
Oriental Mindoro		
Calapan City, Oriental Mindoro	Nath RC Lagpar	09654937748
Palawan		
Palawan	Jenelyn Tabinga	09058368411
Puerto Princesa, Palawan	Yede Mode	09386056220
Puerto Princesa City, Palawan	Kristine Harrison	09512377631 / 09533758590
Romblon		
Romblon	Harold Sembilon Miñasa	09691346561

Region V – Bicol Region

Albay		
Daraga, Albay (Daraga Bakery)	c/o Sir Nelson / Panadero Yan	-
Ligao City, Albay	Gues Tuason	09208310075 / 09164578776
Polangui, Albay	Esteban Sañosa	09957856413
Tabaco City, Albay	Martha's C/o Sir Phil	-

Camarines Norte		
Daet, Camarines Norte	Charlie Oajeng	09305114851
Daet, Camarines Norte	Ukto, Jaz	09283081917
Labo, Camarines Norte	Raffy Otazo Dax	09076403748
Paracale, Camarines Norte	Maluka Maria Perpepo Buena	09770848675
San Vicente, Camarines Norte	Ling Cortez	09224024018
Camarines Sur		
Bombon, Camarines Sur	Evelyn Bento Balloyer Heraty	09081671104
Canaman, Camarines Sur	Luz Monica Parte Esmeralda	09103473119
Iriga City, Camarines Sur	LEning Ning	09090673394
Magarao, Camarines Sur	Alvin Manuel Delva	09319170327
Minalabac, Camarines Sur	Fabie Arejola	09195920724
Nabua, Camarines Sur	Jabodep Dinero	09462185351
Naga City, Bicol	Monding Ella	09483737746
Naga City, Camarines Sur	Maisbel Bodel	09463376667
Ocampo, Camarines Sur	Rolando Espinosa	09395178322
Catanduanes		
Catanduanes	Jose C Jimenez	0968-625-3817
Masbate		
Masbate City, Bicol	Roselyn Berouda Bejda	09978815013
Tagbon, Milagros, Masbate	Joly Z Brippo	09468727227
Sorsogon		
Sorsogon City	Noel Biglena	09260162438

CAR – Cordillera Administrative Region

Baguio		
Baguio City	Maybelle dekos Santos	0917 720 6750
Mountain Province		

Mountain Province	Charlene Donga-el	09568514596

VISAYAS

Region VI – Western Visayas

Antique		
Patnongon, Antique	Ruel Magana	09109389562
Capiz		
Capiz	Tingje Herrera	09512099680
Roxas City, Capiz	Jaja Bond (Jaja Mano)	09619200722
Iloilo		
Iloilo City	Michael Po Lim	09178616453
Alimodian, Iloilo	Leo Bernasol	09206195517
Negros Occidental		
ARAAL partly area of Bago City and La Carlota, Negros Occidental	Alexis Cahilig [Area Coordinator]	09461439367
Bacolod City, Negros Occidental	Matet Lozada / Thesa Riova	09212027644
La Carlota City, Negros Occidental	Narciso Padasas	09066015330
San Enrique, Neg Occ	Ely Carpepo Ciapela	09616079934
Talisay City, Negros Occidental	Eric Moxso	09216860590

Region VII – Central Visayas

Bohol		
Bohol	Violeta Betucas Plotpo	09433493987
Clarin, Bohol	Celso V. Carmosa	09639019063
Cebu		
Carcar, Cebu	Lyndon Villegas	09173077447

Carduman, Mandaue City, Cebu	Algie Gabini	09478523831
Cebu City	Benja Cabacis-Ruiz	09205267166
Lapulapu City	Arlene Jumangit	09393344236
Liloan, Cebu	Romeo C. Arpaparago	0956 507 8765
Minglanilla, Cebu	Glen R. Quitayen	09171503841 09497450832
Naga, Cebu	Jeannette Monte Allubas	09058170232
South Cebu City	Nic-Nic Climaco	09260828011
Talisay City, Cebu	Renaldo Arpacin	09560094880

Region VIII – Eastern Visayas

Leyte		
Brgy. Catiraan, Ormoc City	Carolon G. Alipiabon / Cam Lon	09637706269
Northern Samar		
Rosario, Northern Samar	Edwin Acido Deniña	09380352698
Samar		
Calbayog City	Ruby Gallang Laure Regina Tabula	Regina: 09177223043
Calbayog City	Ricardo Maghacot III	09639231883
Catbalogan City, Samar	Eppag Emmanuel	09757565395
Southern Leyte		
Hinundayan, Southern Leyte	Marichu Cantero	09171276716

Region IX – Zamboanga Peninsula

Zamboanga del Sur		
Pagadian City, Zamboanga del Sur	Marichu Asis	09282859011
Tukuran, Zamboanga del Sur	Marik Adyac	09669201772

MINDANAO

Region X - Northern Mindanao

Bukidnon		
Valencia City, Bukidnon	Joel Abernasca	09979077907
Misamis Oriental		
Magsaysay, Misamis Oriental	Basilio Gerona, Jr.	09067975334
Cagayan de Oro		
Cagayan de Oro	Aureliano Villahermosa Sombilon	09955633195

Region XI – Davao Region

Davao City		
Davao City	Jun Calaps	09159584988

Region XII – SOCCKSARGEN

Cotabato		
Kabakan, Cotabato / Kidapawan City	Rolando Suarez Leonora Suarez	09282542288

Region XIII – Caraga

Butuan		
Butuan City	Edward Tabaquag	09185802205
Surigao del Norte		
Surigao del Norte	Jamar Delara Gaviga	09951958586
Surigao del Sur		
Surigao del Sur	Charlene Montenegro	09630770766

OVERSEAS

Dammam, Saudi Arabia	Aigag Bernal	0569335758
New York City, USA	Elvira Galang	3478735166
Overseas	Ruby Japara	-

OOOOOO

17
Update - Sunday, Sep. 4, 2022
Homily – Clairevouyers

We may not believe the power of clairvoyance or the ability to read the future but people still seek fortune tellers especially before the beginning of the new year.

They go to these so called street fortune tellers using tarot cards or those who do palm reading or even Chinese soothsayers who read the future.

Why do gullible fall for this kind of glib talkers who are out to fleece them?

Many world and business leaders are known to call on these psychics who become their regular political and business advisers.

History is full of these psychics. Prophets are known to be one of the early predictors of ancient Israel. They even predicted the coming of our Lord Jesus Christ and his life and death . Then came Gypsies who use crystal balls. Then the Chinese fengshui experts who read the future every Chinese New Year.

And the famous clairvoyant is Nostradamus, who was an astrologer, a physician and a seer who accurately predicted the future in his poetic quatrains. He wrote this in 1500. Remember the assassination of President Kennedy and the World Center attack. Those were predicted by Nostradamus.

What about the Philippines? There was one video tarot reader who before the May election predicted a candidate with good intention will not win and the candidate with bad will win the presidency . True or not ?

Believe it or not? We are no Ripleys and many of these soothsayers make false predictions and many can be called modern witches or those misguided elements who are just out to make their own fortune from our misfortune.

With regard to these clairvoyants, I have had encounters with them when I was still young. In college, there was a campus fair and there was a booth where a Pakistani student was making some money from palm reading. Out of curiousity, I decided to walk in and lo and behold he told me after reading my palm, I should shift my course which I didn't disclose to him because my destiny was to be in business. Well, I didn't shift but I ended up taking masters course in business. Then another clairvoyant I was introduced to by a common friend asked my name and my birthday when I was still looking for a job, and he accurately predicted I would be working for a multinational bank and he even named FNCB which is called Citibank afterwards. He also told me I would go up the ladder and I would be sent abroad by this bank. Well, I got accepted by FNCB after I passed the test and I rose from the ranks, underwent executive program and was sent to US for training. Furthermore, he predicted I would be an owner of bank which also happened when i negotiated for the purchase of a bank and became its president. Unfortunately, the bank was sold and I never wanted to be a banker again.

Then another lady Chinese clairvoyant in Baguio who was selling Chinese iching when I was browsing in her store and she asked me to come forward and she held my two earlobes and suddenly she said I am a generous person and very humanitarian and she predicted I would be successful in my career and money was not going to be a problem and I will be joining the government as I have much to contribute because of my experience and knowledge and my heart to serve . What ? That period was when Philippines was still under martial law . And I was just an ordinary clerk in Citibank .

These clairvoyants didn't predict I would be an IT man and I relied on my own ESP which is what really mattered to me as my forte was in making bank programs.

But then I didn't realize also my expertise and experience in IT would prepare me for this investigative work we are now doing to resolve the fraudulent election and to uncover the truth.

While on this subject of our sleuthing with my colleagues, another clairvoyant was making prediction that we would succeed and this will come before year end.

Wow? I wouldn't rely on this clairvoyant.

My personal belief is that it's okay to make your predictions or destiny but you should work hard to achieve your personal success. Those predictions are merely circumstantial or coincidences and I believe and trust first in the Lord rather than these mortals who boast about their wares of predicting the future.

Remember what I described here in my wall about making predictions . The late columnist Doroy Valencia wrote : "Don't predict anything unless it has already happened ".

Friends, enjoy your Sunday and don't seek clairvoyants as you are the best clairvoyant of all. We make our own destiny because that's a gift from God and pray to Him as He alone knows what's best for us and for our country.

May the Good Lord of Truth open the door for us so we will see the light once again shining in our country.

Amen .

ooooooo

18
Update – Sept. 9, 2022
Mystery Novels

From the time I opened my Fb page to public after the May election and came up with my own questions on possible irregularities, I first raised the manipulation of the transparency server which broadcast to the whole world in the first hour that the election was over.

One of my followers started to chronicle my posts from that day to this day and is coming up with a book about these posts as if this is history in the making. He shared with me excerpts of his book and I can't share the book without his permission. After I read his compilation, I was amazed that from the posts I wrote for the past couple of months, the book of posts has the making of an Agatha Christie, Sherlock Holmes, John le Carre, and Graham Greene and even Ian Fleming stories combined.

I asked myself how and when the ending of these posts will occur?

I have to admit that my daily posts have occupied my time to the point that when I fail to post a message or two on any given day, some of my friends would pm me and ask me when I am going to write my post for the day. Well, I didn't know that I will be pressured to write daily until some of my close friends reminded me that I already have thousands of followers. I didn't expect this as I don't count myself as an influencer nor a blogger which gives me negative trademark. I am a teacher and also a preacher as I always end my post with a praise of glory to the Lord . This is the motto we learned from our Ateneo upbringing - Ad Majorem Dei Gloriam (AMDG). In English, for the greater glory of God.

To all my followers and those I may have disappointed that if I don't post anything for the day, I beg your indulgence that I cannot accommodate all your friend requests. The positive part from these public posts is I have learned from all of you and you have changed my silent advocacy to a radical advocacy to get to the bottom of this election mess. Your reactions and contributions to the ideas on how tackle this election case helped me and my team to pursue without letup to uncover the truth.

In my last post, I mentioned that we are about to close our investigation which began with our series of questions on the election hoax, from the untruth about the transparency server, the manipulated sd cards, the sale of sd cards to candidates, the manipulated random manual counting, the law of large numbers and the constant ratio of election returns, the presscon at Kamuning bakery, the interview with abs cbn, the summit meetings at Christ the King, the UP Hotel and Marikina fora, to the relentless truth petition campaign from online to written petitions to the Comelec, the CAC and JCOCAE.

The final leg of our investigation is the unanswered letter request for the transmission time stamped date from Comelec in the first hour. Unless and until we get the answer, we will not be able to connect all the dots to the election crime.

But like all fiction and non fiction books about spy novels, there will always be a good ending as the good always triumphs over evil .

We shall wait for the outcome of our letters which have to be answered by these regulatory authorities. A trip to the SC cannot be discounted but the last resort rests with the million disenfranchised voters who can exercise their legal right to redress their grievances.

This is political history.2 in the making not the fake movie MIM. I am sure it will not be a happy ending for the illegitimate incumbents.

May the Good Lord save us from the election poison heaped on us by these criminal minds.

oooooo

19
Update - Sept. 18, 2022
Hiding the Truth

We just received this copy from one of our truth warriors who bravely wrote Comelec following our recommendation to bombard Comelec with the same communication we wrote comelec which to date remains unanswered.

This is the nth comelec reply to many letters emails sent by our team truth warriors.

The comelec reply is a standard or templated reply which doesn't directly answer the request.

So, if this trend continues, then we can only assume comelec is hiding the truth from the million disenfranchised voters.

Do we allow them to get away with this evasive templated response?

Huli na nga tinatago pa Di ba ? Ayaw pa mag kumpisal . Wala naman kami sinasabi na ka kasuhan namin sila ah?

Sige tuloy tuloy lang sulat at email ang Comelec . Kung umabot daan daang padala po niyo, sigurado Meron sa loob mapipikon na at sasabihin na ang totoo.

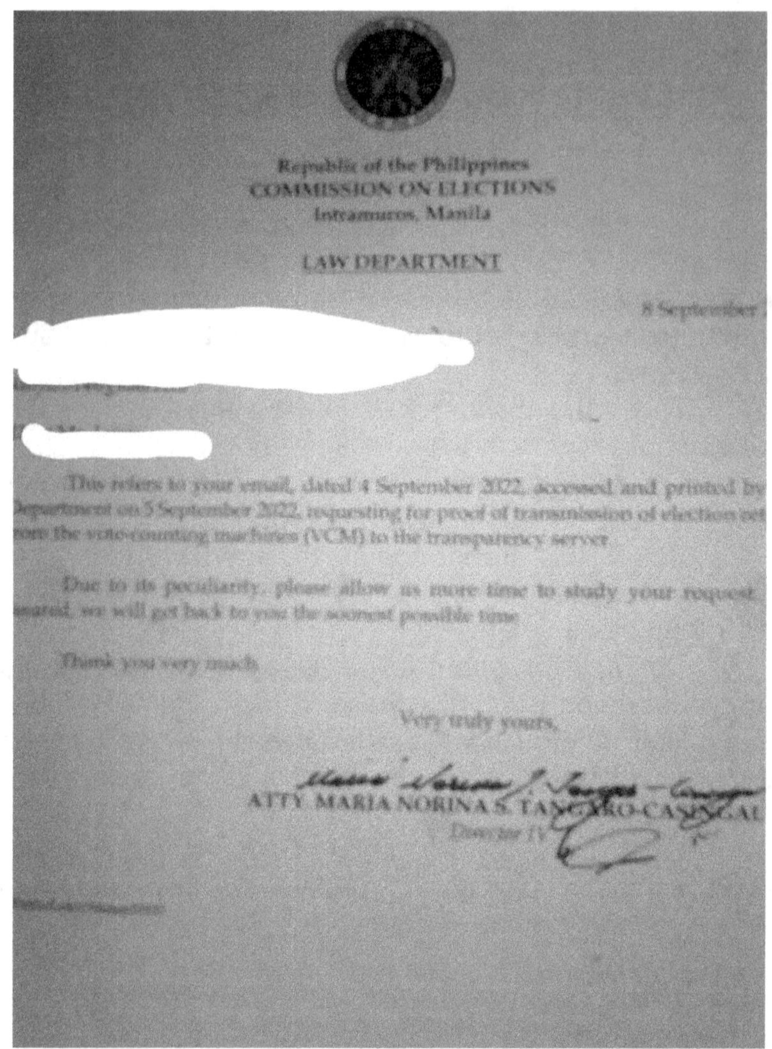

Republic of the Philippines
COMMISSION ON ELECTIONS
Intramuros, Manila

LAW DEPARTMENT

8 September

This refers to your email, dated 4 September 2022, accessed and printed by [the] Department on 5 September 2022, requesting for proof of transmission of election [results] from the vote-counting machines (VCM) to the transparency server.

Due to its peculiarity, please allow us more time to study your request. [Rest] assured, we will get back to you the soonest possible time.

Thank you very much.

Very truly yours,

ATTY. MARIA NORINA S. TANGARO-CASINGAL
Director IV

OOOOOO

20
Update - Sept. 19, 2022
On One's Faith

In one of pms I received, there is one who acknowledges my life dedication to our Blessed Mother. He also acknowledged he belongs to another faith. But I did not engage in theological or philosophical discussions about faith because I am not a priest neither am I one who can compare faiths of people .

While we were born and raised as Catholics, this doesn't mean we are dominant in religion. After the last ecumenical council, the church already opened its doors to other faiths and since we offer the same prayers to one God, then we are no different from each other.

But I stand guard against obtrusive approaches of certain missionaries or those who publicly profess Catholicism is not true church.

Just checking in one passages of a bishop martyr who was about to be executed by a Roman emperor. The emperor told him if he brought in all the wealth of the church his life will be spared . So the following day, he brought all his faithful and he said these people are my treasures. He was still beheaded.

And other purveyors of untruth about faith where they claim the Catholics idolize Blessed Mother and they claim this is blasphemy . I don't engage in any religious debate and in my hometown at the town plaza, there are ministers from different faiths debating endlessly why their faith is the true faith and you can only be saved if you join them.

Really? I must admit many Catholics abandon their faith because they don't find meaning in the way the church handles peoples lives. In fact, amongst secular order, they accuse the priests of robbing Juan for every sacrament. Many may not know this but secular priests depend on their faithful kindness and they don't force them to give any donation unlike one faith that practices titheing where a portion of your pay goes to the church.

Anyway, for more than 2000 years, the church built their center of adoration in Vatican City and around this city you will find many churches and catacombs of martyrs under St Peter Square. I have been through these historical sites and I just wonder how and what kind of lives did Christians go through their martyrdom.

The church teaches us for every blood of Christian, another Christian is born. Well, I don't know the answer either.

But going back to my friend and follower who believes in our truth advocacy, I give due respect to any person whatever belief they have. I can't be the judge of people if they do not belong to my faith as I am sure there many Christians in name only and after each service, they go back to their criminal activities,hueteng, racketing etc .

The door to heaven is wide open but if you keep yourself out of the door by committing offensives against God and His Son and His mother, then it's not the church who is in trouble but you are.

I am sure when we all die, St Peter will not bother to ask us if we are Catholic, Protestant, Muslim or even atheists kasi doon sa langit Malalaman nitong atheists na Meron palan God.

So in our advocacy, while I profess my faith and dedication to Mama Mary, it doesn't mean my faith is my savior. Hindi po.

Katotohanan po Hanap natin Hindi faith po. Problema lang ang mga kalaban natin ang Faith nila ay PoWer at Pera !!

Hindi sila mananalo sa dakilang faith natin na katotohanan .

oooooo

21
Update - Sept. 19, 2022
Trips abroad

Why do illegitimate leaders embark on world tour after their questionable election?

Simple. Because they know they didn't win the election and their election was based on fraudulent means.

Since they don't have full acceptance of their constituents, much less the non existent 31M but true 14M and even more than that, their incumbency and rule will forever be marked with full doubt and they will not get cooperation from whatever they want their people to do or to follow.

Hence, since they don't have such full recognition or acceptance as the legitimately elected leaders of the country, they need to go to the outside world to convince them to accept them as the country's legitimately elected leaders.

The Asian trip and now the UN trip are just disguises to tell the rest of the world that they are the true representatives of the Filipino people .

Question is : will the rest of the world leaders accept them. Being invited by these world leaders is a good indication just like Cory who was given standing ovation in the US Congress when she visited US. But inviting yourself and be accepted amongst the lineup of world leaders is not the right way. You will just be pariah amongst these leaders . Remember Digs when he attended one Asian conference, he was being ignored like a fly or a mosquito. He was not a welcome guest because of his maladministration and bad human rights records. In the case of the incumbents, their win was not convincing to world press and world leaders made known their incumbencies are still in question .

Our role is to validate what world leaders already know that we don't have legitimate leaders.

No wonder, they are rushing gargantuan budget approvals not to mention their bloated intel funds which are non accountable to the people . This budget is for 2023 and we pray we won't see this daylight before the end of the year.

oooooo

22
Update - Sept. 20, 2022,
10AM NYC
Mandamus Petition to SC

Kanina po umaga kahit maulan, I played with my fellow UP Alpha Phi Beta brods in the south.

It was meant to be a pleasant game but after 9 holes, lighting was flashing and the course had to announce game is discontinued . While resting in the lounge, the subject of my advocacy came up and here are some highlights.

If we have such proof of no transmission in the first hour, then Comelec will have to give convincing reason why and how they managed to pull that magic of 20M. Given that, Comelec will find ways to delay and delay their answer to our request.

They asked me to document all communication regarding this request for transmission data as the comelec's response will always be to exhaust all legal remedies except to disclose the requested transmission data.

Now, if we decide to bring this matter to the Supreme Court, the fight there is much different. Yes we may have such legal and sovereign right to request Comelec transmission data but the government lawyers (Solgen) will defend the case and will keep on postponing and postponing the case up to even 6 years.

As suggested by my lawyer brods, get our top caliber brod lawyers as we have in our roster Brods who were former Justices like CJ Reynato Puno and Associate Justice Quisumbing . We need outstanding election lawyers who can defend our mandamus petition so the SC will grant our request. We know many SC justices were appointees of Digs but we understand there are some infighting between the two camps already . We don't want to speculate on that but we will count on the patriotism of these justices so the whole country will know the truth. This cannot be left open to speculation anymore . We will present transmission reports that show there were no transmissions made between 7 and 8.

Thanks to my lawyer brods and the lull in thunderstorm which stopped us from playing gave us this opportunity to discuss legal options .

Marami pa legal options but won't take them up here.

I missed the boat when I had an opportunity to be a lawyer as my mother refused to send me back to UP law and forced me to find work to help pay for the tuition of my two sisters who were still in school.

Well, I have banking and computer mind, legal mind I am still learning.

Hopefully we will be able to get the top legal personalities from my fraternity.

oooooo

23
Update, Sept. 20, 2022,
10PM NYC time
Transparency Lack

Over the last couple of months, we #TNTRio have gone through many processes of investigation to unravel the irregularities and on Saturday, we will give our responses to Comelec's lack of transparency as mandated by AES law.

We persevered in this advocacy and we sacrificed our time to pursue the truth behind the 2022 election fiasco.

In the Saturday forum, we will no longer pursue other concerns we raised during our presentation to many fora. We will answer line by line Comelec's lack of respect for the mandated law for transparency.

Then we will focus on the outstanding request for transmission data which to date has not been truthfully answered. In due course, after we requested our followers to send same letter requests to Comelec, the response was almost the same with a template that the request is peculiar and it will take them time to answer the request.

But, to your and our dismay, we read some of your responses where you have given up the fight and you are encouraging our compatriots to leave the country for better opportunities.

There is no question in this present dispensation our aspirations for better lives are pfft. With rising prices, higher forex rates, higher unemployment, extravagant and unaccountable budget, some of you have opted to leave the country once again as you can't expect better times under this dubious duo .

Yes. We are aware of your concerns. This is the same feeling that my siblings and friends felt after the assassination of our hero Ninoy in 1983. They left the country hurriedly for better opportunities in the new world.

When Cory won after the edsa revolution many of my friends returned but when Erap, GMA took over they decided to move out again. Then when Pinoy became president, they returned only to leave when diabolic Digs won.

Come 2022, when VP decided to run against the defeated VP, millions of her supporters, many coming from overseas, were coming home in droves hoping for new life from her.

Disappointed again because of the apparent cheating in the last election, decisions are ringing to once again give up our country.

During all those crises we mentioned , we never left the country and we are determined to fight for the rights of every Filipino.

We figured out this is a case of millions of freedom loving Filipinos against a few destructive malfeasants who maneuvered the last election to favor their winning.

Yes. You all agree they didn't win but we are not giving up our fight to the last breath because we are doing this not for ourselves but for our children and grandchildren.

There will be no more repeat of smartmatic fiasco nor of Comelec negligence or cover up in the 2025 and 2028 election.

Help us in our fight against this smartmatic/ Comelec Corona Covidus Virus as the only antidote to this virus is your faith that the truth will prove us right.

Please bear with us and if we still fail, then you can go and find opportunities in other countries.

We promise you we will not fail.

May God of Truth keep us together in this fight against false gods.

oooooo

24
Update - Sept. 21, 2022
11AM, NYC time - PPCRV – (Parish Pastoral Council for Responsible Voting)

NAMFREL-LENTE were the only organizations who received legitimate copies of these.

Msgr. Pantin, in behalf of the TNTrio, may I request if your kind office can please ask Chairperson Ms. Myla Crespo-Villanueva of the Parish Pastoral Council for Responsible Voting (PPCRV) to share with us the copies of at least the Transmission Reports (TRs) they have received during their own canvassing at the UST Centennial Auditorium?

A typical transmission report shows the date/time stamp when an Election Return was transmitted by a precinct's Vote Counting Machine (VCM). Gen. Rio wants to expound on his premise that it is impossible to transmit 1,525,637 votes on the first 17 minutes of canvassing, more so 20,061,691 votes on the first 62 minutes, because of the printing speed limitations of the VCMs. I believe that PPCRV should have been furnished a complete duplicate of all ERs and TRs that COMELEC had utilized in their own canvassing, as shown in the Transparency Server.

FB Link of Gen. Rio's Post:

https://m.facebook.com/story.php?story_fbid=pfbid0hi8xas8buK3oe3czqqNwkAo4ksQb7dUAxRA5sE4yTS9WdQgVpzNm1bksrnCX3P...&eav=

9:48

NAMFREL-LENTE were the only organizations who received legitimate copies of these.

Msgr. Pantin, in behalf of the TNTrio, may I request if your kind office can please ask Chairperson Ms. Myla Crespo-Villanueva of the Parish Pastoral Council for Responsible Voting (PPCRV) to share with us the copies of at least the Transmission Reports (TRs) they have received during their own canvassing at the UST Centennial Auditorium?

A typical transmission report shows the date/time stamp when an Election Return was transmitted by a precinct's Vote Counting Machine (VCM). Gen. Rio wants to expound on his premise that it is impossible to transmit 1,525,637 votes on the first 17 minutes of canvassing, more so 20,061,691 votes on the first 62 minutes, because of the printing speed limitations of the VCMs. I believe that PPCRV should have been furnished a complete duplicate of all ERs and TRs that COMELEC had utilized in their own canvassing, as shown in the Transparency Server.

FB Link of Gen. Rio's Post:

https://m.facebook.com/story.php?story_fbid=pfbid0hi8xas8buK3oe3czqqNwkAo4ksQb7dUAxRA5sE4yTS9WdQgVpzNm1bksrnCX3P...l&id=1026127023&eav=

9:48

canvassing, as shown in the Transparency Server.

FB Link of Gen. Rio's Post:

https://m.facebook.com/story.php?
story_fbid=
pfbid0hi8xas8buK3oe3czqqNwkAo4
ksQb7dUAxRA5sF4yTS9WdQgVpzNm1b
ksrnCX3PxLl&id=1026127023&eav=
AfbKY4enEj5lEPeHVGFSV2HoFfzM2b
EpYYh5ntw2_
Oy7OLvCJqKHZ828EMhNveC0gnc&m_
entstream_source=timeline&paipv=0

Thank you for your time and attention, and hoping for a favorable response from CBCP's Permanent Council and PPCRV to help us ensure that our recent election was transparent and fraud-free.

Sincerely,

(sgd.) _______________

Ma. Asuncion Q. Hipolito, MD
PMTER, Core Member

Eliseo Rio Jr
post Aug...

W Doc

Through the diligent assistance of one of our truth warriors who assists the Church as part of her advocacy, she forwarded this letter to Bishop Pantin re : request for ppcrv to provide us copies of transmission reports from vcm during the first four after the May 9 election.

Please take note that we have been getting some copies from certain parties already and the time stamp of transmission data are nowhere during the first hour.

Since the ppcrv is an accredited poll watcher, it is the beneficiary of these transmission data or reports.

We appeal to the patriotic duty of the church which oversees ppcrv operation to share with us these thousands of transmission data to prove whether there were really transmissions made from 26,000 vcm to the transparency server during the first hour where 20M votes were counted already in favor of the incumbent. Thus far, our copies do not show they were time stamped between 7 and 8 but only after 8 and the numbers peaked during the 10th and 12th hour.

We pray we can count on the duty of the church to help us find the truth as we are being given run around by comelec.

oooooo

25
Update – Sept. 24, 2022
Cavaliers' Letters (Military)

Am sharing this powerful message from a follower, a former military man, to his fellow cavaliers as he enjoins them to band together to support the truth behind the May 9 election. The message was reaction to our colleague DICT Usec Eli Rio, a retired Brig General and former UP Vanguard corps cmdr when he delivered his article which we reposted here "was May 9 election rigged."

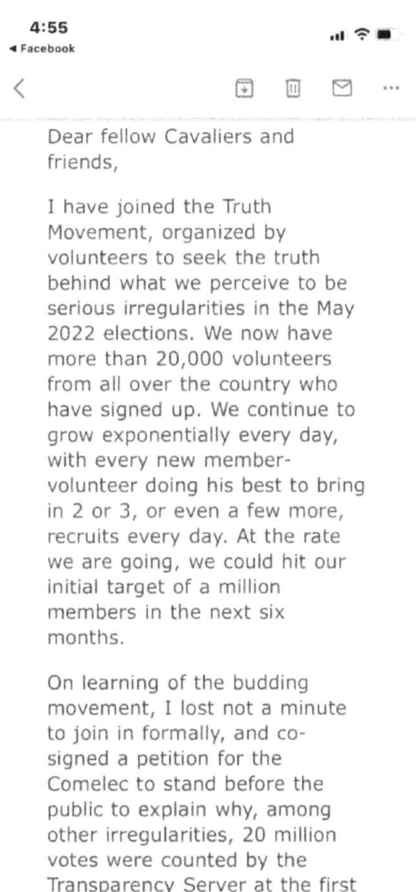

4:55
◀ Facebook

Dear fellow Cavaliers and friends,

I have joined the Truth Movement, organized by volunteers to seek the truth behind what we perceive to be serious irregularities in the May 2022 elections. We now have more than 20,000 volunteers from all over the country who have signed up. We continue to grow exponentially every day, with every new member-volunteer doing his best to bring in 2 or 3, or even a few more, recruits every day. At the rate we are going, we could hit our initial target of a million members in the next six months.

On learning of the budding movement, I lost not a minute to join in formally, and co-signed a petition for the Comelec to stand before the public to explain why, among other irregularities, 20 million votes were counted by the Transparency Server at the first hour of the counting from 7pm to 8pm, ~~and only 13.2~~ million committed perjury when (we can assume) he attested in his COC to his not having been convicted of a crime involving moral turpitude.

We will not mind those who would rather stay in their comfort zones and do nothing. But in the face of what we see as gathering clouds of a risk of the erosion of our democratic institutions - it has started with the unchecked violations of our electoral system in the 2022 election cycle - we in the movement, with your support, are prepared to compel the Comelec to address formally the issues our leaders have raised, and do what else we need to do. I have clear options in my mind to suggest to the leaders of our movement that we do, should Comelec officials opt to just stay put.

I have this lingering notion that our "elected" President may not have the moral authority to govern. The election that catapulted him to the Presidency was, in all likelihood, rigged. He

has been convicted of a crime involving moral turpitude and must have been ineligible ab initio. His followers insist that he was "elected" with a huge majority and we lesser beings must respect "the will of the people". I ask: Didn't the Supreme Court rule in a similar argumentation in the past that "qualifications prescribed for public office cannot be erased by the electorate alone" and that "the will of the people as expressed in the ballot cannot cure the vice of ineligibility"?

And so I pose to all this serious the question: What do we Filipinos do, to right a grievous wrong? The movement, I will stand in support of what the Filipino says we should do.

I ask of you all my friends, to please lend your support to the movement and its mission.

God save our benighted land!

Ding Odono
PMA '64

no question at all on the
position he has taken publicly.

Please know that Eli, together
with other senior leaders of our
movement, has officially written
to ask the Comelec to formally
explain to the voting public
those highly improbable election
results. We have had no formal
reply from Comelec, which leads
us to presume Comelec may not
even be able to make any
attempt at cover-up at all. For
reasons that appear obvious to
my mind: the Comelec officials
were grossly incompetent or
were complicit in those
irregularities, or both.

At least two Senators and quite
a few other people have said we
must now put the election
controversies behind us, move
on, and let BBM do his thing! I
would think our movement could
move on later when its work is
done, but must do its thing for
now: seek the truth and hold
those who violated the law
accountable: the Comelec, over
the election irregularities, and
BBM himself who could have

votes counted in the second hour. That single fact alone of "mathematically, logically and statistically HIGHLY IMPROBABLE if not IMPOSSIBLE results", quoting Retired General Eliseo Rio, Jr. who wrote the attached paper, and other election irregularities, should convince concerned Filipinos among us that the May 9, 2022 elections may have indeed been rigged.

Our Eli, as you may know, is an exemplary UP Vanguard, an electronic engineer who was formerly a Commissioner of the National Telecommunications Commission and a former Undersecretary for Operations of our DOTC who headed the Department as OIC later. I have had the privilege of working with Eli since the lead-up to the May 2022 elections and I have not the slightest doubt that he stands on moral high ground when he says to all who cares to listen, that the elections may have been rigged. His paper, attached, has details clear enough to ~~explain why I~~ have

OOOOOO

26
Update, Sept. 27, 2022
10PM NY Time -
Meaning of Mandamus Petition

On my own, I did research on the meaning of mandamus petition which we will file before the Supreme Court. Let me share with you my findings.

I will need opinion of our lawyer followers to comment and share their comments on this matter . We need volunteer lawyer followers who will help represent us in court.

Here are my findings:

1. What is mandamus petition ?

A writ of mandamus is a remedy that can be used to compel a lower court to perform an act that is ministerial in nature and that the court has a clear duty to do under the law. When filing a petition for a writ of mandamus, you must show that you have no other remedy available. A writ of mandamus is different from an appeal.

In our case, we are filing this mandamus petition to the SC to compel the Comelec to disclose the transmission data to us as we have no other remedy. Comelec has not categorically answered our letter request and has not given us due course. Instead, they referred us to CAC and JCOCAE and we communicated also to these two bodies and we were not given direct answers too. This petition is going to be ministerial in nature as the SC will simply ask Comelec to disclose the transmission data to us. In short, this may be given due course by the SC which will request Comelec to respond to our request.

2. Who can file for a petition for mandamus?

Mandamus is a "special civil action brought by an aggrieved party against a tribunal, corporation, board, officer or person unlawfully neglecting the performance of an act which the law specifically requires as a duty resulting from an office, trust or station".

In our specific petition, we, the registered voters, are the aggrieved party because it is our constitutional right to information about the conduct of the election. More specifically, we are only requesting for the disclosure of the transmission data which are available in the comelec's computers. This info is relevant because Comelec released result of 21M votes in just an hour after closing of voting and we want to know the source documents how the 21M was counted.

3. What is a writ of mandamus Philippines ?

A (writ of) mandamus is an order from a court to an inferior government official ordering the government official to properly fulfill his official duties or correct an abuse of discretion .

In our specific case, the Comelec refused to categorically answer our request and has neglected its official duty to disclose the transmission data which are available in their computer. Said request is not contrary to any existing law and we are citing our legal right to know the basis for the early transmission of result.

4. Is there a time limit for filing of petition ?
I found none.

5. How much does a mandamus cost?
I found none.

6. What is a cause of action for mandamus?

A mandamus action is a lawsuit that is brought against the Government, not for money, but to make the Government do something that it is required to do.

In our case, we are not asking for sums of money. We are simply asking the SC to compel another government body to do what we are legally asking them to do and that is their legal duty to disclose to us the transmission data.

7. Can a mandamus be issued against a court ?

Mandamus. "Mandamus " means " we command ". It is issued by the court to direct a public authority to perform the legal duties which it has not or refused to perform. It can be issued by the court against a public official, public corporation, tribunal or inferior court or the government.

In our case, we are raising the petition before the highest court because if we file the case in the lower court, then this may be appealed to the highest court which is the Supreme Court. Our lawyers want to file this directly to the Supreme Court because the decision is not appealable although the government can request for MR or motion for reconsideration.

8. What happens after writ of mandamus is issued ?

After a writ of mandamus has been successfully acquired and filed, the Government has a certain prescribed period to respond to the complaint. In other countries, it's sixty days.

9. How do you file mandamus petition ?

Since there are three of us as complainants we will have to file individually our judicial affidavits.

10. What are judicial affidavits?

Judicial affidavits shall contain sworn attestation at the end, executed by the lawyer who conducted or supervised the examination of the witness to the effect that He faithfully recorded or caused to be recorded the questions he asked and the corresponding answers that the witness gave .

11. Are judicial affidavits necessary ?

Yes. The Pangasinan complainants have yet to complete their judicial affidavits which are written in several copies. We will do the same.

12. How important are judicial affidavits?

Judicial affidavits become the basis for the case, providing basic information about the facts of the matter and outlining the nature of the case. This document is part of the court record maintained on the case and can be inspected by anyone reviewing the record.

13. What is counter affidavit?

It is an affidavit by the other party in opposition to the one already made.

14. What will happen if the respondent in a complaint does not submit his counter affidavit ?

If the respondent does not submit his counter affidavit, the investigating officer shall resolve the complaint based on the evidence presented by the complainant.

We believe the comelec will respond to our petition by submitting its counter affidavit . Such affidavit must refute our statements or allegations which contain our evidence and proof.

There are many rules or court procedures when you file complaint against persons.

In my own personal experience, I went through all of that and since my complaints involve sums of money I have to pay docket fees. If the case is criminal there are no filing fees. In our specific case, this does not involve sums of money. Hence, there are no filing fees required.

After we file the petition together with our judicial affidavits with the SC, the matter will be closed to the public. In which case, the case will be subject for the deliberation by the SC and the litigants. Discussion of the case outside the court is prohibited as the case is considered sub judice, which means, the legal matter or controversy is now under the jurisdiction of the court. Nobody, including the press and other media, should interfere by publication or public clamor with the court's proper handling of the proceeding . Otherwise, the court can file contempt cases against such persons who violate the sun judice rule and there are penalties for this violations.

Therefore, while we are on the subject of filing this petition, we are still free to discuss the case.

And for our volunteer lawyers and followers, we would need your services if you are available.

Meanwhile, we are preparing our judicial affidavits which will contain basis for our complaint or request. This will be a lengthy affidavit complete with proofs and evidence, including communication letters to Comelec, CAC and JCOCAE and other pertinent exhibits such as transmission reports we have on hand. We shall also include option to compel the telcos to proceed us transmission data in the event Comelec refuses to grant our request.

For your info.

oooooo

27
Update, Sept. 29, 2022
8PM, NYC – No Politics

Even as we inform you of our action and we listen to your comments, we would like to mention here that our filing of the case is not political and we clearly stated that in our affidavit.

Hence, we don't want the court to know that we are representing any political party . Otherwise, our case may be considered an election protest. We put that in our disclaimer .

So let's refrain from mentioning here any political persons who can lawyer for our case. We have dropped lawyer names who have political affiliation including top lawyers or justices. This is not easy for us but we will get the best legal minds who follow our objective. Some lawyers backed out just like those press people who do not want to be entangled in possible threats of closure.

When our chips are down, we believe we will get tough lawyers who will not back down just like us. Since we are only IT and private citizens we won't materially benefit from the case.

It's the truth that will hurt people who hide it from the disenfranchised voters. We speak on your behalf.

Pray for us and our country and the next generations so this won't happen again.

oooooo

28
Update - Oct. 1, 2022,
9AM, NYC time – Strong Dollars

This post was shared with me from an article which appeared in the western press and was carried by local news.

I have said this before and I will repeat this in this post.

True. As they say when the US sneezes the whole world catches cold. US is battling against heavy inflation after it pumped billions of its currency to prop up its economy. Even as we write this, US is spending billions more to support the Ukrainian war machineries in its fight against Russia.

Let's not forget that US is the biggest market for world trade. It is the largest buyer of goods from all over the world. And countries like China, Korea, Japan, Taiwan which produces billions for American consumption cannot afford to use all its excess dollars from its exports. To balance its economies, China expanded its excess dollars by investing in third world countries to make it one of the big competitors in the world. It lent billions to countries who cannot afford to pay them. Take Sri Lanka , African and South American countries. China Silk Road is directed to countries which are dollar short and could not afford to build infra in their countries . One by one these counties defaulted on their loans andChina has no choice except to take over those facilities they built . But China in the end loses what it has invested in these host countries. Further to this, China keeps its excess dollars in US government securities and all counties with surpluses keep their excess dollars in these securities which keeps the economy going. In other words, US, the biggest buyer of all products , doesn't care whether it prints all billions of its currency as it ends up also on the other side of their balance sheet. That's why US can always threaten countries as it can freeze their assets if these countries take up negative action against US interests and its Allies. US froze Iranian,Iraqi, Afghan and now Russian assets in US dollars . The mighty dollar always reigns in the world and it couldn't care less about its inflation as it hits the rest of the world .

Now for developing or third world countries like Philippines which I explained is always a deficit ridden economy and which doesn't produce oil and is heavily dependent on imports . It cannot survive unless it encourages foreign direct investments and inward remittances from its overseas Filipinos . These inward figures are not enough to offset the country's import requirements. At the current state of affairs, the incumbent cannot stop the outflow of investments because of the precarious state of the Philippine economy. With the dwindling number of its international reserves, expectation is dollar will hit 65 or even 70 before end of the year.

I mentioned this before and I will mention this again. Philippine peso doesn't react alone to worldwide inflation . Traders or finance people always look at the sovereign risk of each country . Investors will not come in unless they know they can get out at the quickest moment.

Now, where does the Philippine economy stand now ? Investors are still wary of the political hold of these incumbent leaders who have not even lifted their fingers nor can they get their acts together to stem the outflow of dollars . Nobody can guarantee that the current leaders can hold on to their power long as their acts of fattening their fiscal emoluments or budgets will leave the economy in tatters .On the fiscal side, this government wants to print more pesos to fatten budgets of the two leaders at the expense of sacrificing the needs of the country's essential needs like education, health, food and other important economic benefits. Crowdsourcing their budget will mean the country's growth will be impeded and investors won't have the confidence of keeping their investments or putting more monies into the country .

Does anybody care now that on the fiscal side alone, government borrowings which finance the budget deficit will hit almost 20Trillion even before the budget is spent next year?. We need to stop this bleeding.

It's the economy, stupid, says this American candidate.

We can't expect this incumbent nor its economic team to fix our economy if they just want to fatten themselves at the expense of the general public .

Hence, brace yourselves for more downfall of the Philippine peso for as long as these leaders just continue to mind their own pockets rather than the stomach of millions of Filipinos .

NEWS.ABS-CBN.COM
US dollar an unstoppable force endangering other currencies

oooooo

29
Update, Oct. 7, 2022,
9AM – About CBCP and PPCRV

Our group has been reaching out to CBCP and its designated citizens arm, PPCRV, which is responsible for ensuring honest conduct of elections. We were specifically requesting for copies of transmission reports during the first hour after closing. We obtained some copies from ppcrv poll watchers but we specifically requested for more than that figure.

We already communicated to CBCP and we received non conclusive support as they referred us back to ppcrv.

Ppcrv has not been cooperative enough despite our requests. Many of our truth warriors who we requested to send the same letter to ppcrv have not received any positive responses.

After checking the role of ppcrv, its responsibility is to ensure election is honest and credible. But at one point we cited them for not raising alarm about the questionable transmission reports. In fact we received reports about some volunteers being axed for questioning the election process.

The connection with the CBCP has been established as it was chosen to be the citizens arm to protect election process.

Now why are CBCP and PPCRV stonewalling us?

If they are not responding to citizens call for giving us copies of transmission reports, then their role is put on the line.

If we don't receive responses from our requests soon, then we shall be constrained to refer this matter to our legal team to ensure we get their support.

https://en.wikipedia.org/wiki/Parish_Pastoral_Council_for _Responsible_Voting?fbclid=IwAR3-JVQOp8BloRC25U6CgBj011o9uJuPLewjqdY8pAp1zegl OCZvdIVPDzU – copy and paste - **Parish Pastoral Council for Responsible Voting**

From Wikipedia, the free encyclopedia

oooooo

30
Update, Oct. 7, 2022 –
7PM NYC
Something fishy about the CBCP and PPCRV
And the Runaround tactics.

What's on the mind of CBCP when they replied like this to one of our truth warriors who was only asking for their help in getting transmission data from ppcrv which is affiliated with CBCP.

I have been trying to connect the good governance part between ppcrv and the CBCP.

It is obvious that with the response by CBCP to our truth warrior that ppcrv is an autonomous body with its own board, it doesn't have a say on the governance of ppcrv.

When the late Cardinal Sin and some religious and lay leaders established the ppcrv, they adopted the name parish pastoral council for responsible voting. Two words, parish pastoral. These words imply the CBCP has moral jurisdiction over the body it created . If the intention was to create an independent autonomous citizens arm, then it should make a statement that, henceforth, it should not allow the two words, parish pastoral be the prefix for this body.

It's a shame that the founders who had good intentions when they established this body during the time of Cardinal Sin, we, the citizens, cannot even get the attention of CBCP and it's affiliate ppcrv.

Hence, let it be the case, that, we citizens, will express our disinterest in the ppcrv as the future citizens arm as it's not the true representative of the people.

What happened to Namfrel which was dislodged as citizens arm ?

I used to be a Namfrel volunteer during the 1986 snap election.

Make your judgement after reading this reply from CBCP.

6:28

Franklin's Post

12:33 · 87%

← **Fw: People's Movement for ...**

Dear Ma'am Hipolito,

Greetings! We are in receipt of your email sent to CBCP General Secretary! On behalf of Bp Colin, our Chairman, we thank you for this pursuit for truth in the last electoral exercise!

Since PPCRV is an autonomous lay entity which has its Board, we suggest that you address your request directly to the PPCRV leadership! We can only encourage and appeal for the sake transparency! They are copied with this email! Thanks

Fr Tony

On Fri, Sep 30, 2022 at 1:02 AM Ason Hipolito <asonhipolito2004@yahoo.com> wrote:
    September 30, 2022

    BISHOP JOSE COLIN M. BAGAFORO
    Chairman
    The Episcopal Commission on
    Social Action, Justice and Peace

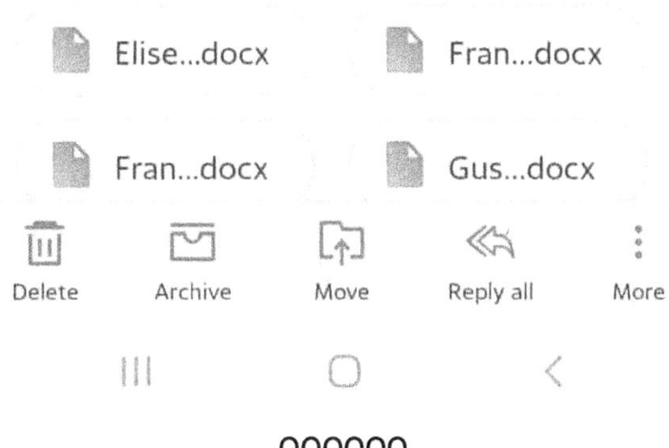

12:19   89%

←   ATTN: Msgr. Bernardo Panti...

In this regard, we would like to ask the help of the Catholic Clergy to bring awareness of this serious problem to your respective dioceses' parishioners. As their shepherds for a just and truthful way of life, the Filipino Catholics look up to your sound and moral guidance, which help us choose enlightened actions to most mundane or dire problems.

May we ask for some precious time of the CBCP Members to listen to the forensic evaluation of the TNTrio regarding this apparent electoral fraud? Please help us bring TRUTH and JUSTICE to our people and the generations to come.

Kindly contact us if the CBCP Members, hopefully, accept our plea and the date the congregation will be available for the meeting/presentation.

Attached are some of the social media posts of the TNTrio with regards this issue.

Thank you very much for your kind accommodation of our humble request.

Respectfully yours,

(sgd.) ----------------------------------

(sgd.) -----------------------

MA. ASUNCION Q. HIPOLITO, MD
    CRISTINA G. MENDOZA

PMTER   Core
Member   PMTER
Treasurer

Elise...docx   Fran...docx

Fran...docx   Gus...docx

| Delete | Archive | Move | Reply all | More |

||| ○   ‹

○○○○○○

31
Update, Oct. 8, 2022
NYC 11AM – Letter to Truth Warriors

To all truthwarriors,

Re CBCP/ PPCRV request for sharing of transmission data with us.

We requested as early as September 8, through one of our truth warriors said matter and you have read all communication and follow up by our truth warrior and CBCP response.

To avert any kind of wrong imputation on the CBCP/ PPCRV, the reason why we are asking them is because the ppcrv is the citizens watchdog for responsible voting . We just like to get their cooperation even if we have received already some from certain quarters. This will help bolster our mandamuscase which we have been preparing already for more than a month.

We are gathering enough proof and evidence whether there were really transmissions made on the first hour . What we have are transmissions after the first hour which we showed you.

All CBCP and PPCRV has to do is to confirm with us they don't have such transmission data during the first hour . That's all.

Is that so difficult to do?

Mahirap po mag prepare ng case just like the Pangasinan case. We are spending on our own to pay legal fees because this is not a simple case.

Plus the fact that we can't afford to file the mandamus case later than November 9 because that's the sixth month after May 9 election holding period of CDRs by telcos. If we are able to file the case before that date we will also file with SC to compel telcos not to delete the logs.

We cannot be disclosing our movements to all as we are working deep with our lawyers exploring all possible avenues to lock in with our mandamus case and to get the answer from Comelec about the transmission data.

Pag Wala transmission during the first hour, then the broadcast of 21 M votes counted is erroneous. Pag Meron then we close our case.

So, I encourage everyone to refrain now from making further comments against CBCP and PPCRV and I will delete my posts within the day about the exchanges between CBCP and our truth warrior. We have already done our share and if they don't cooperate we cannot compel them.

Kayo na bahala kung Makakatulong kayo sa pag kuha ng transmission data from PPCRV.

Maraming Salamat po.

oooooo

32
Update, Oct. 9, 2022
NYC time, 9PM - Faith in our Cause

Let me share with you a personal true story which happened many years ago when I was the head of treasury of a bank.

During the merger of the bank with a couple of financial institutions, I was tasked to head the team and I had to temporarily leave my post to my deputy.

During that period, my deputy committed serious mistakes when he took positions in forex and kept those positions from me and after one month, when I asked his positions, he claimed to have squared his positions. At first I wanted to believe him, then I asked for accounting reports. The chief accountant showed me the books and I found certain multiple forward postions, in traders' terms these are called swaps. I checked them out and they were interbank forward transactions and I was surprised the magnitude of these transactions as these were not commercial transactions which are normal banking transactions. Now, from traders point of view, taking forward positions means the trader is hiding his positions. These swaps involved selling currencies spot and buying them forward with points representing interest differential.

To help you understand how these transactions work, let me explain these so when you check out banks' financial statements, look for contingent accounts which are shown below the balance sheet. These forward transactions are not booked as current. These are called FXB or FXS, forward exchange bought or forward exchange sold.

Then when you examine the forward rates, you can dissect that the trader bought certain currencies at spot rates and when the rates move against the spot rates, the trader covers his position by buying forward at at certain future. When you do this, the other bank who sells you this forward currency will compute the interest differential between the two currencies and add the differential result to the spot rate. This is a cost to the bank. When the forward matures then the bank has to buy back his currencies and will book the interest cost.

When I traced all these spot and forward transactions, I called on my deputy to explain the forward transactions and he tried to evade my questions. After I showed him the books of forward transactions, he bowed and admitted he had to cover a potential loss. Then I told him to unwind his forward positions to cut his losses.

The bank had to shoulder losses from these transactions after the forward contracts were canceled.

When I reported these losses to my superior, he couldn't believe what happened.

Then my superior turned around and presented to the board that I committed trading errors which caused the bank huge losses. He wanted to sacrifice me to save his neck. He even went so far to visit me in my residence with a letter of resignation for me to sign and admit my wrongful judgements. He tried to offer me amounts and position with other banks. I refused.

Then, the bank's board called for full

Investigation and even invited the Central bank to audit all the bank's transactions.

During that investigation, I was kept in the dark and I was already worried about my career and that I would be blacklisted and I won't be able to get another job.

I panicked and I was suffering from sleepless nights and before I almost suffered nervous breakdown, I turned to prayer to Blessed Mother. I prayed rosary non stop while the investigation was on going.

At the end, after the investigation, I was exonerated by the central bank and they didn't find transactions that gave me financial benefit.

When my superior was tasked by the board to explain why he should not be sanctioned, he defended his position that he didn't know what was going on in treasury and he came to know about the losses when i reported this to him.

He wanted to burn me before the board and one director asked me if I had any piece of document to show that my superior knew about forex transactions.

I scrounged for my files and since I always made regular reports to him about bank positions, I found one document where in that same report, he signed noted and that gave him away when I sent a copy to the director.

After the investigation, the chair called me and told me the decision of the board. I accepted the decision and I submitted my resignation but I was not penalized and he gave me clearance and I was not blacklisted. My superior was sanctioned and was asked to resign.

What does this prove to me and to our case before comelec ?

My personal case proved that documents matter and our case before the comelec will prove that documents will matter.

That's the reason why we are asking for copies of transmission reports which are public records from poll watchers, from political parties, from ppcrv and will also call with court order on telcos to provide us CDRs. These transmission reports will prove whether there were transmissions made on the first hour to prove there were 21M votes counted.

We pay importance and relevance to documents as the court will not accept any hearsay defense.

After my bank stint, and when I went to my software business, I encountered clients who didn't pay after I delivered the software. I presented signed contracts when I filed civil case against my clients. I won 100 percent all my cases.

This comelec case is no different from my collection cases. Together with my colleagues under #TNTrio, we are confident we will win our case with documents on hand plus our mandamus to secure from comelec and telco validating documents.

We need your vigilance and prayers for miracles to our Blessed Mother who never left me when I was under investigation. This time powerful miracles will happen to relieve all of our concerns regarding irregularities in the last election.

Mama Mary, intercede for us to your Son Jesus Christ to secure the truth.

Amen.

oooooo

33
Update, Oct. 11, 2022
NYC time, 130PM – Personal Banking Experience

Let me share with you a personal true story which happened many years ago when I was the head of treasury of a bank.

During the merger of the bank with a couple of financial institutions, I was tasked to head the team and I had to temporarily leave my post to my deputy.

During that period, my deputy committed serious mistakes when he took positions in forex and kept those positions from me and after one month, when I asked his positions, he claimed to have squared his positions. At first I wanted to believe him, then I asked for accounting reports. The chief accountant showed me the books and I found certain multiple forward postions, in traders' terms these are called swaps. I checked them out and they were interbank forward transactions and I was surprised the magnitude of these transactions as these were not commercial transactions which are normal banking transactions. Now, from traders point of view, taking forward positions means the trader is hiding his positions. These swaps involved selling currencies spot and buying them forward with points representing interest differential.

To help you understand how these transactions work, let me explain these so when you check out banks' financial statements, look for contingent accounts which are shown below the balance sheet. These forward transactions are not booked as current. These are called FXB or FXS, forward exchange bought or forward exchange sold.

Then when you examine the forward rates, you can dissect that the trader bought certain currencies at spot rates and when the rates move against the spot rates, the trader covers his position by buying forward at at certain future. When you do this, the other bank who sells you this forward currency will compute the interest differential between the two currencies and add the differential result to the spot rate. This is a cost to the bank. When the forward matures then the bank has to buy back his currencies and will book the interest cost.

When I traced all these spot and forward transactions, I called on my deputy to explain the forward transactions and he tried to evade my questions. After I showed him the books of forward transactions, he bowed and admitted he had to cover a potential loss. Then I told him to unwind his forward positions to cut his losses.

The bank had to shoulder losses from these transactions after the forward contracts were canceled.

When I reported these losses to my superior, he couldn't believe what happened.

Then my superior turned around and presented to the board that I committed trading errors which caused the bank huge losses. He wanted to sacrifice me to save his neck. He even went so far to visit me in my residence with a letter of resignation for me to sign and admit my wrongful judgements. He tried to offer me amounts and position with other banks. I refused.

Then, the bank's board called for full

Investigation and even invited the Central bank to audit all the bank's transactions.

During that investigation, I was kept in the dark and I was already worried about my career and that I would be blacklisted and I won't be able to get another job.

I panicked and I was suffering from sleepless nights and before I almost suffered nervous breakdown, I turned to prayer to Blessed Mother. I prayed rosary non stop while the investigation was on going.

At the end, after the investigation, I was exonerated by the central bank and they didn't find transactions that gave me financial benefit.

When my superior was tasked by the board to explain why he should not be sanctioned, he defended his position that he didn't know what was going on in treasury and he came to know about the losses when i reported this to him.

He wanted to burn me before the board and one director asked me if I had any piece of document to show that my superior knew about forex transactions.

I scrounged for my files and since I always made regular reports to him about bank positions, I found one document where in that same report, he signed noted and that gave him away when I sent a copy to the director.

After the investigation, the chair called me and told me the decision of the board. I accepted the decision and I submitted my resignation but I was not penalized and he gave me clearance and I was not blacklisted. My superior was sanctioned and was asked to resign.

What does this prove to me and to our case before comelec ?

My personal case proved that documents matter and our case before the comelec will prove that documents will matter.

That's the reason why we are asking for copies of transmission reports which are public records from poll watchers, from political parties, from ppcrv and will also call with court order on telcos to provide us CDRs. These transmission reports will prove whether there were transmissions made on the first hour to prove there were 21M votes counted.

We pay importance and relevance to documents as the court will not accept any hearsay defense.

After my bank stint, and when I went to my software business, I encountered clients who didn't pay after I delivered the software. I presented signed contracts when I filed civil case against my clients. I won 100 percent all my cases.

This comelec case is no different from my collection cases. Together with my colleagues under #TNTrio, we are confident we will win our case with documents on hand plus our mandamus to secure from comelec and telco validating documents.

We need your vigilance and prayers for miracles to our Blessed Mother who never left me when I was under investigation. This time powerful miracles will happen to relieve all of our concerns regarding irregularities in the last election.

Mama Mary, intercede for us to your Son Jesus Christ to secure the truth.

Amen.

oooooo

34
Update - Oct. 11, 2022
NYC time, 6PM - What about whistleblowers

Remember the PDAF Queen who was arrested after her nephew whistleblowed on her as the mastermind. She detained her nephew after she found out he nephew was stealing her business of running after legislators who are seeking her favor for commissions.

After his relatives sought help from NBI and finally had him released, the nephew exposed her activities.

What followed next was indictment of the PDAF Queen.

In the case of former press Secretary Trixie who whistleblowed about troll payments, and after the former ES was asked to go, can we expect train of whistleblowers from those disgruntled former officials who supported the incumbent.

We are on the threshold of filing our own mandamus case for Comelec to show us transmission reports during the first hour after polling closed and where 21M votes were counted.

Amongst the #TNTrio, after we read the comelec reply to our truthwarriors similar request, we believe they exposed their weakness and perhaps after our pressure on the case, one or two whistleblowers will come out and prove whether there were transmissions made during the first hour.

Wouldn't we all believe that after all our prayers, slowly something positive is unfolding supportive of our cause.

Let's continue praying to the Holy Spirit who has repeatedly guided us in this effort to unearth the truth. May God help us and lead us to the finale we want !

Amen.

oooooo

35
Update - Oct. 12, 2022
NYC time 6PM – Our Case for Truth Improving

Mukhang gumaganda ang ating kaso para sa katotohanan.

Sa tulong niyo nakita natin ang palusot ng comelec.

Tapos Yung mga nawala sa circulo sa palasyo nag umpisa na mag laglagan.

Hindi lang yan. May balita na Yung malaking tao na nagbigay sa kampanya at hindi nakuha ang pwesto malapit na rin mag bulgaran.

Marunong talaga po ang Diyos . Pinakikinggan tayo.

Kaya may kasabihan Sa African proverb, " When elephants fight it's the grass that suffers!l

Tapos tungkol naman sa mga thieves " Is there honor amongst thieves ?" Sabi ng kaibigan kung police detective, " pag nahuli mo ang isang magnanakaw, sigurado kakanta yan kasi malungkot siya kung siya lang nakakulong".

Kaya tabi muna tayo at hayaan natin sila mag WWF.

Pagkatapos tayo naman Pasok sa eksena ng katotohanan.

Translation to English

Looks like our case for truth is improving.

With your help we found the excuse of comelec.

Then those who were lost in the circle in the palace started to fall.

It's not just that. There's news that the big person who gave in the campaign and didn't get the position will soon be vulgar.

God really knows. We are being listened to.

Kaya may kasabihan Sa African proverb, " When elephants fight it's the grass that suffers!l

Then about the thieves " Is there honor among thieves ? "My friend who is a police detective said," if you catch a thief, he will surely sing because he is sad if he is the only one in jail."

So let's step aside and let them do WWF.

Then we enter the scene of reality.

oooooo

36
Update - Oct. 13, 2022
NYC time 700PM – Brave Lawyers

What can we learn from the past 5 months about our campaign?

I was reclusive in my fb limiting my audience to my friends without entertaining followers at all.

What drove me to open up is because I couldn't stomach the fate of the country with election results during the first hour from Smartmatic automation giving dubious and spurious and unbelievable results.

As banker / IT with combined 50 years of experience, spewing out that kind of 21M in just the first hour is highly unacceptable and questionable.

But what drove me to go deeper is because my siblings and my children were all crying and asking Why? Why! Why?

I didn't know much about automated election but when I saw the graph of a UP analyst, I told myself that's a very simple process, a four step process and my banking software is 100 step process.

Really? That smartmatic people is not smart at all. Yes, they may have fooled non IT people but they can't fool us.

Then when I started my sleuthing based on how we develop systems, I immediately concluded this smartmatic is after all a fishy or a cheating machine.

How can you really produce 21M in less than an hour from thousands of precincts all over the country unless the so called transparency server was pre programmed.

The series of questions I asked myself led me to put up on my private page and then some of my friends started to push me to go further and farther with my evaluation.

I posted that the machine is like your laptop and there's an app that you open and the app tells you the process and if you follow the process you get the results. That's it.

But what if the app is designed to create a result which is not logical because computers are more logical than human minds. But if they are logical, then there should be no errors. When we develop programs, almost always when we test them, the results don't come out right because the logic of the system is erroneous. Hence, you find errors on the screen and then you go back to check your codes.

It's that tedious and long hours of work to work on a simple program.

Now, can machines and apo be programmed to produce results even if you follow the process? Yes. Some IT pundits have demonstrated that when you press A and the letter will show B. Just two lines and you get the opposite.

You see. Logical pa rin.

So, I assembled my programmers to validate whether if you insert your ballot and you check or shade the name of the person you are voting for, can you program that it will be read and counted in favor of the other person?

They answered in unison - Yes, boss. So, I asked them to go ahead and wrote the codes. Result : the shaded votes were counted in favor of the other candidates which were not shaded. Simple . Yes. They just give commands to the system that when the system sees and reads shaded name of that person, counting command will be given to the other person.

Going back to the election results, I figured that somebody must have toyed around with the smartmatic system. But why wasn't this observed and seen by the political parties or obsevers when this was tested.

Well, the smartmatic programmers must have more than one SD card or secure data card like a USB which contains data of voters and candidates and the program itself.

If the correct SD were used, then there should have been a correct process of counting the ballots. But what if there are several SD cards with different set of programs and methods of counting? Then you don't get correct results .

This led me to conclude that that the process itself can be flawed, and the transparency server could not be transparent at all because the smartmatic programmers made sure the actual votes in the ballot boxes which are not opened and are never manually counted cannot be the basis of the manipulated SD in the VCM.

When I went public in my findings, I began to receive comments, some supportive and some unsupportive. I received many friend requests but I couldn't accept them because i only accept requests from my family members, close friends and classmates. Then, followers grew and there were many shares made about my findings.

After a couple of days, a large business group whose president is a good friend invited me to explain how I arrived at my findings. He said he was following me and I obliged.

In that meeting attended by his board members who are top businessmen, I met Gus Lagman and Eli Rio who were also invited and were requested to present their findings.

When we looked at our presentations, we found out that the missing dots in our investigation became connected.

And the business group couldn't accept the election result and they didn't issue any congratulatory system unlike other business groups and associations which issued such statements.

What was really unbelievable was what Eli Rio presented about the constant ratio based on the published results from the transparency server.

There began our association, and we were invited by friends from overseas when they learned about our findings.

We made cohesive case presentation before the press and other fora.

We continued to pursue the truth and Eli Rio, former NTC commissioner and former DICT Usec , made effort to check the data which produced the 21M votes. And that's where we remained focused now as on hand we don't have transmission reports from some sources who were beneficiary of ERs and transmission reports showing there were transmissions made.

Now, going back to our connection with Pangasinan case, the Media reached out to us and invited us to present our findings because the Pangasinan voters couldn't accept the results. More than 100k Pangsasinense petitioned comelec to open ballot boxes and manually count. This was rejected by comelec and even their appeal for reconsideration was rejected. This was people power and not politicians who were clamoring for their rights to know the results by opening ballot boxes and manually count.

Then, one of the Pangasinan candidates spoke to me about the SD card and he said before the election, a person connected with smartmatic and comelec offered him a chance to win if ha came across. His proof was SD card. Wow! He said after he read and saw my description about how SD card can change election results, he came to me. He was leading in the pre election polls 70 in his favor and the final result showed 70 against him. He didn't come across. Then when I shared this story in my page, many messaged me that also happened to their candidates in their provinces.

Now, it's time to restore our faith in our election system. When many countries dumped automated election system including smartmatic, back to manual system is the new method of election.

This present core of comelec commisisoners still want to continue with this system and are even asking for billion budget to buy vcms and it's prepared to defend the automated system in the forum next week and yet it couldn't give us straight answer about showing to us proof of transmission reports. That's why we are challenging them before SC.

We are advancing our case hopefully before November 9 because that's the date the telcos will delete the logs of transmission or what we call CDRs.

We will be writing these telcos to keep the logs until we are able to secure SC order.

We have a good legal team with election lawyers and lawyers who are with us fighting for the same cause.

While we impressed upon these lawyers that the #TNTrio are not the beneficiaries of this mandamus petition, we cannot afford big legal fees if this were an election protest. Modest fees lang we asked them. No worries they told us . Para sa bayan .

We have volunteer lawyers but we were able to raise minimal funds from our followers and contributors and from our own to pay for the services of these lawyers. They are dedicated lawyer friends and I have missed many who I asked to be our lawyers. Unfortunately, many are old already and some have conflicts as they are representing their clients before government. Not easy to get good lawyers.

But through our Lord's intercession, we were able to get these good lawyers who have the experience already in litigation even before the SC. We cannot be represented by lawyers who are lawyers for political parties as we will be tainted and the SC may look at our case as politically motivated.

It's just a simple case according to our lawyers as it's just a mandamus case but facing SC, Solgen, Comelec, we need to be prepared.

Maraming Salamat sa mga abogado po na tumutulong sa atin.

May the Holy Spirit guide them in the case study and preparation.

PS one of the lawyers is a co seminarian who is now a top lawyer and I didn't know that we have many seminarians who found their own different calling like me but we all hailed our God after we ended our reunion a couple of weeks ago with our arms raised - saying AMDG (Ad Majorem Dei Gloriam! For the Greater Glory of God!

Amen to that and may these brave lawyers fight with us for the truth and for our country !

oooooo